MW01286122

Musical Miles

A Journey

Mitch Alden

For Dylan, of course

~ *foreword* ~

In July of 1992, seven of us drove away from the suburban New York home in which I had spent most of my childhood. I'd tell you that we were driving out to Boulder, Colorado, but that was only a place on a map, somewhere we'd heard of and about. It wasn't yet an actual place in our lives. In the years before the internet we truly had a very limited idea of what was out there. In classic early twenties form, we had some camping gear, a bit of clothing, our limited, amateurish band gear, a few cases of our freshly recorded CD, a map or two, and, yes… CB radios.

We had dreams, though, and we thought that would be enough. We were most of a band (short a lead guitar player). We were going to create something big.

I didn't, though, have the others' musical history, natural talent, and confidence. I could say that my entire fledgling music career rested on the one year I had just spent gigging with Mitch and Johnny as a member of On Air, but I really owe it all to the friendship I'd found with them. You see, being anywhere near Mitch means that you're being drawn - compelled even - into what so many of us now call "Mitchy world." This, I had learned early on, is a truly unique place. Simply put, Mitch doesn't believe in boundaries; he doesn't know limits; he sees reality as something that he can shape by choosing to believe in the version of life that he wants and moving forward toward that end. While at times this means that he's been wrong when he estimates how long something will take or delusional as he describes nearly vertical mountain climbs as "hills" to hike up, it also means that he's believed in me, fully, from the very first time we met and then played together in the corner of a strip-mall bar that would have to pass for a stage. It was no different last year while I was unemployed and he constantly reminded me about the power of my perspective or even now as he asked me to help him with this book. His writing this and my working with him on the edits was just another in a long line of "of course we can do this" events. Yes, I was on board with this project from moment one, which is the same thing I said when he first asked me to play music with him and Johnny and we then moved across the country a year later.

It's this faith from him that I had bolstering me as we left for Colorado, and it was there as we played endless amount of gigs together for seven years. Even though I don't play music anymore, the confidence I gained while doing so with Mitch has been with me as I've gotten married, launched and maintained a career I love, learned to move forward since my parents' passing, and as I work to raise my amazing kids, who love their "Uncle Mitchy" and his music. Over these 22 years, we've climbed many mountains together.

If you're reading this, I'm psyched for you because it means you're about to spend some time in the world that Mitch continues to build, a creative and bottomless world of potential, a world where it makes total sense to run long distances, play music, and go scuba diving (Mitch's latest full-time hobby) in the same day. It's where an adult can be on stage performing and scream "Wee-hoo" and "What fun" into the microphone and people don't doubt the sincerity of his joy. It's a world gripped by optimism, a place you probably wouldn't bother reading about in fiction because it would seem implausible, a place that I hope will intrigue, amuse, and inspire you the way it still does for me and so many others.

-Dave Hochheiser
November 2014

"Change is the only constant in life."

~ Heraclitus

Nerves

The pink sun glanced off the tips of the skyscrapers making their dark forms look like candy. The enormous early morning crowd moved with an electrical fluid motion towards the race's downtown starting area as if it were one focused and unstoppable collective nerve impulse.

"Bag drop off to the left, starting corrals to the right, qualifying runners only beyond the gate," chanted the uniformed officer as the thousands lined up, said goodbye to loved ones, snapped pictures, and made post race meeting plans. In just under thirty minutes, fifty thousand runners would embark on simultaneous twenty-six-point-two mile adventures through the streets of Chicago. As the anticipation of the blast of the race's start horn grew exponentially in each runner's nervous belly, a shared enthusiastic restlessness seemed to reverberate among them in ways similar to a pinball forever erratically bouncing against a machine's high score sweet spot, the manual flipper bumpers never needing to be used.

Mitch shuffled along the sidewalk as nervous energy poured off of him causing the runner to take off his sweatshirt, wait a moment, and then put it back on. Seconds later, he'd make sure his fuel belt was stocked, and then he'd do it again. Next, his hat would come off as his mind went over his pace schedules. He'd then repeat his hopeful finish goals to himself while he put his hat back on and took off his sweatshirt, each clothing swap a layer too much or too little to achieve perfect comfort.

As Dylan did her best to calm his nerves, he grabbed her hand and continued squeezing it firmly as they followed the designated arrows towards the race's starting corrals, the area where the masses of runners were herded into sectioned-off zones according to their self proposed finish times in order to alleviate a disorganized and dangerous bottleneck at the race's onset. Just prior to entering this fenced off gridded area is where he would finally have to kiss his wife goodbye.

Walking towards the gate, he gave off an aura of satisfaction as he told himself that his hard work and positive focus would reveal the well oiled machine he considered himself to be. His mind, bubbling over with excitement akin to a rambunctious child stepping onto a playground at recess, for reasons he couldn't quite pinpoint, wouldn't allow him to fully commit his heart to the pure joy of the experience. Deep down, fears unknown to him would tease his confidence with doubts and anxiety on how fit and rested he actually was to race the distance.

With a vocal cadence hinting exhaustion, excitement, doubt, and pride, Mitch said, "I can't believe this is all happening. I'm here. I'm psyched, but it doesn't seem real."

Recognizing what needed to happen, Dylan stopped her husband, cradled his cheeks with her soft but athletic grip, and locked his eyes. "You will do the best you can. You will finish strong. And you will run knowing how proud of you I already am."

As he did his best to unclench the nervous fists he held at his side, Mitch, in return, gently raised his tightly controlled and open palms to Dylan's cheeks, kissed her lips, and said, "I know I can do this, but I recorded a CD this week. I poured my heart and soul into my music twelve hours a day for eight days straight. My body feels beat." He paused and then admitted, "I want to run this thing strong, but I can't tell what's left in me."

"Stop Mitch," she whispered. "Just think about the journey to come. You get to experience all the great feelings running a marathon has to offer. And you get to share these feelings with thousands of friends. Have fun with it!"

He gently kissed her again, nodded, told her he loved her, and walked past the officer giving directions.

Once past the runners only checkpoint, the congestion of shoulder to shoulder runners quickly built up as each athlete often changed direction in order to find his or her proper bag drop off booth or designated starting corral, each hundreds of yards from the other with thousands of runners in between. As the electricity of everyone's energy caused those gathered to emit a somatic odor mixed with a garnish of a random runner's Ben Gay, Mitch dropped off his finisher bag at his numbered booth, turned around, and swam through the thousands of other runners in search of his starting spot. Alone, yet among many, his enthusiasm's battle with self doubt and fear continued.

As he slowly zig zagged and meandered with the momentum of the crowd towards his designated starting area, Mitch couldn't help but to tap into the growing excitement and adrenaline of the mass of athletes that surrounded him. By the time he got to the place where he would hear the starting horn blow and finally be able to start running, the cumulative emotions of all those around him helped to inspire the competitive runner within him.

His view was now obstructed due to the crowding in his starting area, and he was only able to see a few rows of runners in front and behind him. He stood comfortably on his small piece of claimed pavement alongside his fellow marathoners. As he chatted and connected with those next to him about racing to the best of each person's abilities, he was finally able to suppress and overcome all of his negative feelings with the strong poise and invincible morale of a six-year old who, for the first time ever, had just ditched his training wheels and began to fly on two wheels around a deserted parking lot.

"I'm gonna kick ass!" rolled reflectively off his lips.

Memories of countless training runs and the past week's recording elicited a huge smile of accomplishment from the musician-and-husband- turned-runner-turned marathoner. *I've trained for months… I made a great record this week, and I've learned so much about myself doing both,* he thought. *Time to push it again and learn some more.*

It was ten minutes to race time.

A Quality of Life Decision

Mitch backed his pickup truck to the load-in dock. The setting late December sun indicated the time was around 3:45. As he gazed at the alpenglow off the crisp new white of the early season's ski hill, surges of adrenaline poured off every inch of his body; the good feeling of freedom was every bit as expansive as the mountains he was gazing at.

As he looked up with squinted eyes towards the top lip of the mountain, he did his best to clearly see the highest chairlift tower and imagine his speedy descent off the first headwall underneath the lift, the imagined gravity paralleling his immediate future's reality. For days to come, instead of driving a desk prior to singing, he would be ripping turns down a mountain or running a blissful pace along the frozen dirt roads adjacent to his home. Unable to contain his excitement, he said out loud, "I quit my job today!" followed by, "So cool that I get to enjoy my days focusing on what I choose to do and then get to rock."

The singer turned, dropped the tailgate of his pickup, and opened the upper door to the bed's cap. First grabbing and unloading his hand truck, he started to let these thoughts roll around in his head.

Did I really figure this thing out? he questioned his own validity as he guided a large speaker to the truck's tailgate, lifted it, turned, and carefully placed it on the portable cart.

Next, a smaller crate of assorted cables was pulled and placed on top of the speaker as he answered himself, *Yeah… I think so.*

Mitch shut the back of the truck, *After twenty years, I think I've finally figured out how to live off playing music.*

Grabbing the hand truck, he shook his head with disbelief and thought about the amount of time he had dedicated to the profitable bottom line of a boss's balance sheet just because he needed a decent paycheck, a real job. But like a dieting sugar addict who pretends to enjoy eating kale, he couldn't fool himself. Deep down, he just wanted to play music. He wanted music to be his job, but he didn't know how to make it happen, until now.

Tilting the loaded hand truck back and then rolling it forward, he couldn't help but think about how long he had lied to himself.

Every hour I put towards my day job sucked an ounce of happiness and a pound of energy from my creative side, my music, he said to himself as the ramp flattened out. *Forty five hours a week of music sucking energy. That's a lot!*

He approached the door with a shrug. *And I convinced myself I could play music four to five nights a week at the same time?*

He let the hand truck stop and tried the service door's strong steel handle. *Yes!* the singer yelled in his head as the door's latch unclicked. *I don't have to walk all the way around to open it.*

He pulled open the door, spun the hand truck around and turned his body towards the door, all with the fluid movement of an act done thousands of times before. While he danced with his gear, he reflected on how often, at his day job, he thought about what it would be like to spend his afternoons running, skiing, or writing music, each endeavor serving as a mind settling harmony played out in song over the night's stage.

Propping open the service door with his hip, he noticed the first corner obstacle of stacked empty kegs alongside piles of discarded broken down cardboard boxes. As he negotiated the heavy hand truck of unsecured gear into the building and around the teetering obstructions, he did his best to keep from touching the booby trap and instigating what would likely be a painful accident.

After clearing the danger, his subconscious continued with the theme of the day as it threw images of enchanted trail runs, hikes, and long, slow marathon training runs at him, each experienced in blissful solitude where he understood himself best, where he conceded with all honesty to himself that if he had to work for a living, his wish was for his music to be his life's work, his legacy.

Weird how this all came to be. Mitch said to himself as he moved his gear along the hallway, smiled, and thought, *And it's not a wish anymore.*

As he negotiated another corner, this time psyched that it was much easier than the first, his mind lingered on the memories of what he had been doing for the past seven years. It amazed Mitch that for such a long duration, he was able to show up for work every Monday through Friday feeling tired from the previous night's late night music venture, give the impression to his co-workers that he was dedicated to his job, and catatonically stare at the bleak cathode rays of his computer monitor while he disclosed, only to himself, the sadness of a wild animal tranquilized and taken into captivity.

Rolling the cart around another corner and operating on auto-pilot as he got closer to his destination, he came to a set of stairs, huffed the speaker and crate up the incline, through the next service door, and into the eighty degree kitchen. He shook his head sarcastically at the the manager's chosen route for musicians to load in their gear. Sweat on his forehead started to break out underneath the wool hat he wore. "Oh my. Warm!"

The singer moved quickly across the floor, through the 'out' door and amongst the crowd of vacationing skiers, each sprawled out enjoying their apres ski food and drinks. A few smiles were exchanged between himself and other skiers before he finally made it to the stage. He dropped his gear, took off his heavy jacket, wiped some more sweat from his forehead, turned, and went back for his second load of equipment.

Exiting back into the hot kitchen through the 'in' door, but this time dressed a little more comfortably, he put his wool hat in his hand, smiled through his light sweat, and followed his route back out the way he came. After nodding to a passing bartender and a few servers, he mentally embraced them as his co-workers, took a lot of joy in this fact, and shifted his thinking to the happiness of the moment and his love for the rhythm of being a local musician; an affection and appreciation for moving gear, setting it up, singing for four hours, breaking it down, moving it again, and reliving the experience afterward on the ride home, always churning around ideas on how to make the next show better.

Out of the building and into the back of his frigid truck to pick up his next load of gear, he felt invigorated by the cold temperatures as well as his state of excitement.

"It's because I became a runner," he said aloud as he loaded his hand truck with another large speaker and his stage monitor. "Everything has become so much easier since I've started running."

As he turned his heavy cart back towards the building, he acknowledged the irony to himself: running, an important pressure valve in adjusting his attitude towards working a full time job, had coincidentally helped him to achieve his breakaway from eight to five life.

Rolling the hand truck towards the service door, he mused about the days when he was a slightly irresponsible, yet musically passionate twenty-something who always avoided a full-time career path. Instead, he chose to work part time jobs in ski shops in order to have more time during the day to hike, ski, find writing inspiration from the mountains, and to party the way a twenty-something likes to party.

Inside the building and tip toeing around the keg and cardboard booby trap for the second time that day, he relived the year when he turned thirty one, swallowed his youthful pride, and embraced the expensive desire to record the songs he had written over the past ten years in order to release his music on CD.

Hat off and sweating again as he moved through the hot kitchen, through the apres crowd, and towards the stage, he reminisced about the dichotomy of putting his energy into finding a full time job in order to raise the cash to record his music, only to later recognize that the corporate pressures and daily workloads ultimately diverted all of his musical creativity away from the passion he was looking to support.

Second load placed on the stage, the singer again turned, glanced over the relaxing and happy crowd, and thought about how he had gotten to this point in his life. It was the day he experienced his major turning point, the day he decided he wanted to be a runner. He felt his pace quicken.

Climbing back into the truck's bed to unload his power amp and assorted soft cases of necessary odds and ends, he went over his first ever days of sitting in his cubicle. He remembered being psyched with not having to put his life on a credit card in order to record his music, but also the nagging feeling that something just didn't feel right.

For the third time that day in negotiating the service door with fluid ease, he recalled the moment at his day job when he had figured out what was wrong. He felt himself grip his hand truck with the stress of how he had sacrificed the daily wonder of being cradled by mountains for the guaranteed income of a real job, a path to earn additional cash.

Arriving at the staircase before the hot kitchen, he flashed back to sitting at his desk, feeling the artificial air coming out of the building's vents, and staring at the deep blue skies just out of reach on the other side of his office window. He had spied a group of runners gliding up the city block, each buoyed by the adrenaline of their shared cadence.

His memory interrupted by a quick hello exchanged with the head chef who greeted him at the kitchen door on his way to the pantry, his recollection continued as he repeated the conversation with his boss about needing an early lunch, remembered the feelings of release as he walked out into the fresh early spring air, and his envy as he looked down the street after the runners, each athlete emitting an aura similar to the groove he felt when he was an hour into hiking up a four thousand foot mountain on a glorious spring day.

Though his wife was a runner and Mitch knew the joy she received from running, it never hit him as a sport that would give him the same satisfaction as climbing a mountain, until his eight-to-five reality forced him to be creative about squeezing the sensation of outdoor bliss into his indoor workday.

Walking back out to the truck to unload his acoustic guitar and a few more soft cases, he replayed the conversation he had with Dylan the night he returned from work with cravings for endorphins and the desire to balance out his day job with hiking. As the musician reached for his guitar, he smiled to himself as he thought about Dylan's delighted reaction when he asked her if it would be a good idea if she could take him running on their next day off together.

With the fourth and final light load of gear quickly brought to the stage and his truck moved to employee parking, he sat in the driver's seat and remembered his first run with Dylan. During their run, he talked about life decisions and sacrifices, how good running made him feel, and how surprised he was at what forty minutes of exercise could do for his outlook. Memories of that first run stayed with him as he locked his truck, stowed his keys in his pocket, and jogged back towards the lodge. "Mmmm, to run," involuntarily left his lips. "Definitely, it's the running that got me here."

The musician slowed himself as he approached the service door for the last time that day. He tried the handle and realized that while in his zone down memory lane, he had let the door shut a little too hard and caused it to lock. *No worries*, he thought to himself. *Running around to the main entrance is more fun. And I won't have to brave the kitchen again!*

Winter layers off and boots swapped out for stage shoes, the singer first took his guitar out of its case. He placed it on its stand in order to acclimate it to the warmer and more humid climate of the room. As he did this, he told the idle instrument, "You will stay in tune and sing like you've never sang before."

The singer then unpacked his speaker stands, put the heavy speakers up on top of the them, and elevated them to their proper height by utilizing his legs and shoulder while using his hands to adjust the tension knobs to keep them in place. As he did this, he imagined himself looking to the surrounding skiers like the Greek titan Atlas holding up the celestial sphere.

Once accomplished, he knelt down to the crate of cables to start the tedious job of running microphone cables, mixing board cables, speaker cables, and guitar cables. As he separated the neatly packed coils in front of him, memories flooded his head of how he and Dylan had shared a tiny eighteen by eighteen apartment, which was really just a small room added onto the rear of a large Maine farmhouse.

Standing up and running the first speaker cable from the power amp into one of the mounted cabinets, he disparagingly shook his head with appreciation for Dylan's tolerating him over the many nights, when offensive tones similar to the sounds of fingernails scraping on a chalkboard, trudged from his immature vocal chords.

Running the second speaker cable to the other cabinet, he relived the runs with his wife and the fun runs which kept his sanity during his mid-week work days. Fitness and breathing control quickly developed because of his running. Myriad nights were spent working on strengthening his voice. Dylan's amazing ability to sleep through anything furthered his confidence, except for those few nights when he was a little too loud and was forced to practice his singing in the bathroom. Eventually, his processing came to the night when he realized that he could actually sing.

Background music for the crowd now playing through his electrified speakers, Mitch turned to run microphone cables and thought to himself, *When I first decided to go corporate for CD cash, I had every intention of hiring a singer for "Transitions."* Microphone and direct box cables now plugged in, he continued, *After seven years of making running my priority, I ended up the lead singer on all three of my recordings... And now I'm getting paid to play my music full time?* He paused, smiled, and concluded, *You gotta be kidding me!*

After hearing music being played over the PA, the club's manager approached the stage and snapped Mitch out of his internal autobiography with a hearty "hello" and handshake. She confirmed Mitch's instructions regarding start & finish times and food & beverage guidelines. Thirty seconds later, she was off to her next task.

His PA fully set up, Mitch lowered the background music, stepped up to the microphone, and began to sound check his voice. "Heyyyyyy Yeahhhhh. Ohhhhhhhhhh wohhhhhh wohhhhhh ohhhhh," cranked through the speakers as he monitored the equalization and the input levels. Now that he was a singer, he always liked to check his voice with a melody instead of the stereotypical "check one-two, check one-two." It felt better to him.

After adjusting a few knobs on his soundboard and replaying his vocal melody through the speakers to the entire room of skiers, he overheard someone say to their friend, "He's got a really good voice." Mitch couldn't help contain his smile as he unintentionally slipped back into his memories of the multiple nightly demos of his voice sounding like a warped record spun on a broken turntable.

As he adjusted the effects level, bass, and treble, he calculated that it must have taken him three to four years of working on his voice at night, struggling through his job during the day, and running as often as he could, in order to feel comfortable enough to test the waters, take center stage with his voice, and work towards creating his current euphoria.

Picking up his guitar to sound check its volume, he unconsciously began to play the song *Now*, the tune he had written several years ago and continually perfected his voice on. He thought about how many thousands of times he must have sang this tune into his amateur digital recorder, always cringing at what he heard on playback, and the one night, just hours after completing his longest run to date, how he sang true, perfect, melodic, and in tune.

As the singer placed his guitar back on its stand and again turned up the background music, he proudly recognized that he defined himself as both a runner and a singer. He gladly admitted to himself that the breath control he had achieved through running worked magic in keeping his voice on pitch.

Running feeds singing, was Mitch's next thought, a thought so enormously filled with positive feelings, he had no trouble in assuming that this is what it must feel like to win a race.

He sighed a deep breath of satisfaction, looked at his watch, and calculated that it was ten minutes to show time. After reminding himself that a cold beverage was the only thing missing from the stage, he stepped off and headed to the bar.

While waiting for his beer, a few folks engaged him in the conversation he loved to have. They asked questions about what kind of music he'd be playing that afternoon, what kind of guitar he had, how many years had he'd been singing, and what songs they'd like to hear him sing.

Placing his beer on stage, Mitch felt a full sense of pride that this was now his job. He was proud that he had kept his day job for seven years, saved up enough cash to record and release three full length CD's, develop a following for his music, grow as a musician, grow as a singer, build a network of clubs to sing at, both with his band and himself as a solo player, and finally, to let his day job go so he could pursue his passions for running and singing full time.

He understood that from an outsider's perspective, his thinking would likely be construed as egotistical and self-absorbed. But he also knew how difficult it was to quit a job which paid good cash, take a large pay cut, re-organize the way he spent his money, all so he could play music for work. Mitch then giggled to himself as his mind emphasized the word "play."

I just gotta live within my means, keep singing, keep running, and never stop loving Dylan, was the thought which next popped into his head, followed by, *I think I just made the best quality of life decision I've ever made.*

Harnessing this last thought and all of the day's good feelings, the singer put on his guitar, lowered the background music, stepped up to the mic, and for the first time in his life as a full-time musician, said, "Hey! My name is Mitch. I'm gonna sing some tunes for you!"

And sing he did.

What's Next?

His footfalls echoed off the crowned pavement, adding to the songs of the seasonal birds. Scents of melting snow and decomposing leaves lifted the runner's pace as winter's hold waned and April's last days lengthened.

The time signature of a jovial waltz, 1 – 2 – 3 – 1 – 2 – 3 – 1 – 2 – 3, matched the stride of the Emmylou Harris tune playing in his head. As the beat played an endless loop in his brain, the musician tried to calculate the pace he was running by keeping in time with the melody.

What was previously frozen, but now a natural culvert of mud, was hurdled by the runner with the electricity of the rising temperatures and the ensuing fervor of spring's goodness. His extra layer, which was reserved for colder days on the road, was tied around his waist and bounced with his running beats.

Gotta start cold. Tis the season! the runner told himself as a smile energized his soul and overshadowed the sounds of his footfalls; he was simply gliding. His arms thrust forward with each stride, punching his body further into a dreamland steeped in the fresh pine smell that was finally freed from winter's bland, scentless, and dark hold. The splashes of puddles, just previously solid masses of frozen dirt, tickled the runner's legs with soft drops of a season's change. His heart rate mellowed as his body became the machine he had learned to trust. His mind left his body to start its rambling soliloquy.

Should I run another marathon? the runner asked himself. The doubtful part of his brain immediately questioned, *Do I have the time to train the right way?* The more confident part of his brain answered, *I just need to make the time!* followed by, *But I need to first tune my body for the four month training journey if I'm going to tackle another aggressive training schedule.*

As he thought about this last statement, memories of the three marathons he had trained for over the past five years began to fill his mind's eye. Thinking about how great it would be for his body and mind to again achieve such a strong endurance level, doubt chimed in against his will: *I know how easy it is to sign up for these races, but I also know how hard it is to follow through when life gets crazy and the high mileage runs, which I never seem to have time for, roll around on the training schedule. I don't know.* He let this statement sit for a few minutes.

Hurdling another new puddle, inspiration for something bigger than just training for a race entered his mind. *I think I need something more than a running goal. It's obvious to me how running goals keep me focused, but I think I need to do something bigger for myself.*

After contemplating what bigger meant to him, the doubtful part of his brain piped in and cautiously asked him, *Am I thinking about setting another personal record? Another all elusive 'PR?' That's hard! Especially since I raced such a strong race during my last marathon.*

Seconds later, the confident part of his brain rebutted his dubious side, *I can always train to run faster, even if it means crossing the finish line with a PR of only a few seconds faster than the last marathon I raced.* Mitch thought about this statement for a few minutes and then said to himself, *I know I can accomplish this by running for the love of running!*

Confidence now winning over doubt, the next question popped into his head. *OK, so what race do I run? Or should I not pick it yet and just start training with hopes a race will fall into place?*

It was then that the runner realized that the song he was pacing himself to had fallen out of his head; he was running at a sprint, all aspects of his elation diminished. Catching his speed the way a small parachute slows the force of a massive dragster, the runner came back into himself to deliberate over his immediate running future and continued with his internal conversation.

Training season for hundreds of fall marathons is about to begin. The finale will be races run by millions worldwide. To again be a small part of one of these events would be so great! He let these thoughts sit. *To participate. To befriend thousands of other athletes as the race course takes me through city blocks, country sides, and coastlines, and ultimately cascades me and all the other exhausted athletes through the finish chute where tears of joy are as inevitable as the medals we earn.*

His pace started to pick up again as he thought these thoughts. *To experience the bliss of mid-race intoxication. To push through the pain of the closing miles. To collapse with the satisfaction of finally being done. To taste the greatest post-race beer ever.* The runner let a few more moments pass and then concluded, *Yeah… I should race another marathon.*

After hitting his route's turn-around point and heading back towards home, he let this bold statement sit for several minutes. Though he assumed this would be the last statement of his conversation with himself, a feeling inside him told him otherwise and caused him to think, *If I'm going to race another marathon, it wouldn't be so I could hit another personal record. It would need a harmonic, something more.*

Involuntarily, the runner's thoughts quickly turned to his music, knowing it also brought him the bliss he sought. Following his footprints in the newly melted mud back towards the way that he came, he acknowledged to himself that he was due for another recording. He had shown his fans, his friends and himself - his harshest critic - that, yes, he could sing, he could write, and he could record.

The amusingly absurd idea of combining two of his greatest joys hit him like lightning bouncing between trees.

I know. I should run Chicago! Matt lives and works there now. But can I really endure recording for days on end in Matt's studio and then turn around and race twenty six point two hard miles? The musician thought through the question while his runner's instinct told him that, once again, he would be biting off more than he could chew. *But it would be a balance I've never experienced before,* the musician argued.

As Mitch continued to debate with himself about how to pursue his next adventure, the song of the season's first Hermit Thrush suddenly resonated through the forest, giving the runner a feeling identical to a divine anesthesia.

Letting the bird's song bring him back to the moment, he said to himself, *Easy.* He listened a few more moments, anticipated the bird would sing again, smiled at hearing the repeated whirling vocal cascades of the small bird, and then said to himself, *I don't have to decide anything right now, but wow... What a fun idea!*

1 – 2 – 3 – 1 – 2 – 3 – 1 – 2 – 3. Emylou again focused his stride. The runner laughed quietly about how his thoughts could wander all over the place while he was in tempo, yet remain so targeted and sure.

It's so much fun to run! he said to himself as he let the sounds of his thoughts trail off while letting the murmurings of the forest overtake him.

4

Self Reflection

Nighttime. It was his favorite part of the day, that is, after he pushed himself this way. As he thought about the morning's interval workout, the afternoon's solo acoustic show on the southern shores of Long Lake, and the evening's full band rock show in Portsmouth, NH later that night, he stared into the bedroom's blackness along the same path that would soon reflect the early sun's first light, his mind relenting to cooperate with his body's desire to chill out, say goodnight, and finally rest. Doing his best to stop thinking about how much exhausting fun he had just had, he instead tried to focus on the sounds of the misty rains as they cascaded through the forest's canopy, the nurturing moisture strengthening the roots it would eventually make its way towards.

"Can I get some of that strength please?" Mitch inquired to no one in particular. Answering for the void in her own brilliant and silly ways, his dog, Roo, spoke a squeaky yawn and returned to her blissful dreams of squirrel chasing, rotating from belly to back as the comment was further emphasized by Dylan's sleep-sigh moan coming from next to him. *Thanks guys, but I don't feel any stronger,* Mitch thought to himself.

Instead of the desire to sleep, what had firmly planted itself in the forefront of Mitch's mind was the realization that, although it was all fun, he might have accidentally over-planned and now needed to follow through on his obligations.

He giggled to himself as he uttered his self-imposed "Groundhog Day" mantra: *run – drive – gig.* His twelve to eighteen hour days now included hard training for the 2010 Chicago Marathon, the pre-production of his new record, and traveling all over Northern New England to gig in order to earn the cash pay for his next CD's recording.

Mitch furrowed his brow in the dark, let his egocentric confidence embrace his happy exhaustion, and allowed himself to give life to his newly self-described title. *It's all good... I'm a music-athlete,* he said to himself. *I'm super tired, but in a good way... I feel good. I just gotta keep things happening.*

His mind then flipped back and forth between the two huge endeavors that awaited him in early October. He greatly wanted to make a timeless record. He also greatly wanted to run a super fast (at least to him) and strong marathon. Fresh off a banner ski season and magical spring, both had seemed possible. Now, as he endured a raspy voice, overly calloused fingertips, and a throbbing shin on a tired body, he wasn't so sure anymore. *I've been here before,* his mind rationalized.

He listened to the rain. Just audible over the meditative drips was his wife's rhythmic breathing working in sync with Roo's. He felt in control of his immediate future, yet he was very aware of how fragile his hold on it was. To strengthen his grip on his confidence, he decided to replay the success he had during the making of "Transitions", his first CD, recorded eight years ago in his friend's Toronto studio.

For six months prior to this CD's manufacturing, Mitch would get home from work and record guitars, bass, drums, keys, and vocals, each instrument's colors mixing themselves on a painter's palate as he worked them into the canvass of his amateur digital four-track recorder. Proving to be a much more time consuming task than the musician initially thought, he would spend hours recording through the night, only to finally mellow out once the sky grew lighter and the need for a few hours of sleep would overtake his music making.

After six months of not allowing himself adequate sleep and finally arriving in Canada and heading into the studio to bring his work to life, he had learned quickly that in order to tolerate the endurance of making a great record, he would need to draw inspiration from a different source: his running and his newly found love of half marathons. He had raced his first half just a short year prior to Toronto and found that the experience had an awakening effect on his persistence; the endurance earned from training for longer races seemed to fuel his energy to record for hours on end.

"Transitions" completed and released, Mitch would then use his time over the next several years to participate in several half marathons, which were run in tandem with full marathons. Each year, standing at the finish line and not being able to run another step past thirteen point one miles, he had repeatedly marveled as the marathon finishers each completed their twenty six point two miles with strength, conviction, and smiles. After witnessing their accomplishments for three years straight and riding high on the adrenaline of each racer who had crossed the finish line, he had finally embraced the inspiration to tackle the longer distance.

But the act of training for and running a marathon had seemed completely overwhelming to him. In order to close the door on the easy excuse to re-neg on the commitment, he had thought that if he could choose a unique race and have to invest money in non-refundable airfare and hotel deposits, he would be less inclined to quit. He had no idea what he was getting himself into, but only knew he had wanted to make running a marathon a reality, a once in a lifetime experience.

Funny how my thought process works, Mitch said to himself as he lay in bed, the rain finally letting up a little. *I start thinking about how I recorded "Transitions" and all of a sudden, I'm re-hashing how I became a marathoner.* This made him smile. He loved how the feelings of recording and racing longer distances could be so complementary, each delivering the same amount of preparation, butterflies in the belly beforehand, and feelings of pride and invincibility afterward. *Running and recording make for fun memories,* he said to himself as he let his mind continue to replay his past.

His research of cool and unique races which he wouldn't allow himself to blow off had led him to discovering the Midnight Sun Marathon, run in mid-June in the town of Tromso, Norway, miles north of the arctic circle, where during the solstice weeks of late spring and early summer, the sun refused to set. To Mitch, it was the perfect first marathon.

The race had turned out to be a very small, yet very large event: three hundred fifty seven runners representing thirty six countries. Here, on a remote island in northern Norway, Mitch was introduced to the marathon culture. Each runner he had spoken with, whether around town, at the expo, or at the start line, had a great story and marathon history. Moreover, each storyteller was more humble than the last.

The small Norwegian Inn he had based himself out of during the race's happenings additionally housed a couple from Munich who had arrived the night before the race "in case we wanted to run it," was how Uve had put it, spoken in his best East German English accent. Just a week before with his wife, Inge, he had run the northernmost marathon in the world, somewhere up in Spitsbergen, Norway, a few hundred miles north of Mitch's race. "Last year, they had to bring a helicopter out on the course to chase the polar bears off," he had commented with a smirk in his eye. "But tomorrow's race is special. There are not many races where the gun goes off at

8:30 at night local time and finishes around the midnight hour with the sun still high in the sky."

As Mitch laid in bed thinking about this conversation from five years ago, he remembered with crystal clear vision, as he stood in the hallway of the Inn and looked Uve directly in the eye and had said, "Midnight hour? This is my first marathon! If I could just finish, maybe by two AM... I'd be extremely happy."

Staring at the ceiling of his cozy home, his wandering mind then resurrected the thoughts of how, for the few years prior to him choosing to race an endurance event, he had grown as a runner, gotten faster, and had progressed at his races. He randomly replayed his 10K's, half marathons, and his marathon relay, the race he had run just before signing up for his Norway race.

This relay had given him the opportunity to run next to athletes he had never thought he'd be in the presence of, let alone at their eighteenth mile. Being the third of four relayers on his team, he had been in awe as he ran alongside the marathoners. He couldn't believe that five hard miles into his seven mile relay leg, runners were running as fast as him, and with eighteen miles already under their belts. He was overwhelmed. Later, at the finish, it brought him to the point of tears. *I wanna be like these runners!* had become his mantra during his winter training and had made itself manifest when the gun went off that spring evening in Norway.

It's funny how my priorities were so different back then, Mitch thought as the strong memories of five years ago provided the night's emotional entertainment. *Speed wasn't even a thought,* he continued. *It was my first time running twenty six point two miles, the last eight being completely in new territory. I had no idea what to expect my body would do... How it would respond... If I could actually follow through.*

The runner continued re-living his growth.

At the time he had started his Norway training, Mitch wasn't very competitive, only goal oriented. He hadn't found a training plan on the Internet or pulled one from a running magazine. He had figured that in order to simply finish, he could run four to five miles twice a week and add a long run at week's end, with the long runs progressing two miles per week until he got up to eighteen or twenty miles; he had heard from some experienced running friends, the way rumors are passed around, that if you could get at least one eighteen or twenty mile run in during your training, you could finish a marathon. Choosing the path of least resistance, this had been good enough for him, similar to the way he convinced himself that a bag of Cheetos and a quart of fructose enriched blue Gatorade could define a substantial recovery regimen. He had been wrong here, too.

Man, I was so idealistic when I trained for that race, Mitch said to himself. *And I thought, "Eighteen miles... That should be enough."*

He exhaled a mocking sigh. *I finished the race, but it certainly wasn't pretty. Still, it turned out to be a lot of fun because Uve and Inge were part of the experience.*

The memory of sitting at the Inn's kitchen table across from Uve and Inge, their smiles huge with learning that Mitch was about to run his first marathon, then brightened in his mind. He could swear he could smell the fresh smells of the Norwegian countryside as a breeze blew through his open Maine window. He embraced the way he had felt while looking at them, sitting with his jaw agape, and experiencing instant friendship. "We are going to run your first marathon with you," Uve said with the tone of a proud parent.

After five years, he still couldn't believe Uve's generosity, fitness level, and humility. "Didn't you guys just run a marathon last week?" Mitch had rhetorically asked them.

"This would be number eighty seven for me," Uve had replied, his accent becoming thicker as he talked about his accomplishments. "Inge isn't far behind as it would be number seventy four for her." He had continued with a tone drawn from the inspiration from what he had just witnessed the week prior. "But this is nothing compared to what we experienced with the fifty or so runners last week in Spitsbergen... The world record holder for total marathons run was there last week! I think it was number fourteen hundred and something for him! Yes, I can run my eighty eighth marathon with you tomorrow. It wouldn't be a problem. It would be great!"

Mitch's memory then jumped ahead to the race. The first two hours of it had gone exactly as he had envisioned, Inge and Uve talking running technique the entire time, coupled with stories of how they had gotten into running. The three of them would then fall into a group of ten to twelve runners, folks from Russia, Sweden, the UK, Finland, and Japan.

He remembered saying to his new friends, "You all are crazy!" Between them, there must have been a combined five hundred and fifty completed marathons.

"No, you're crazy!" the runner from Finland had exclaimed in her wonderful accent, "for flying halfway around the world to a different time zone to run your first marathon at night!"

"I can only imagine what your body's biorhythms are telling you!" the runner from Japan had added.

As he lay in bed with a huge grin on his face, he again felt a boost of confidence as he replayed this experience. He knew that when he had accepted these compliments from these runners, real runners to him, he was wearing a similar smile as the one he was exuding in the night's darkness.

His mind then fast-forwarded him to ninety minutes further on in the race when he had fallen behind his new running friends; the eighteen to twenty mile training rumor had proven itself false. For the last third of the race, he had moved at a pace only half as fast as his starting pace. He was hurting, walking, and, with only a few runners left on the twenty six point two mile course, had found himself very lonely. By mile twenty three, the closest runner to him had been over a half mile in front or behind him.

It was here, after passing the thirty three kilometer sign, that he had looked at his watch. With his mind and body in the midst of tandem breakdowns, he said out loud to his weary self, "OK, it's twelve fifteen at night, around a half hour or so left to run... Wait a minute, it's twelve fifteen at night! What the hell am I doing in northern Norway on some random airport access road running a marathon in the middle of the night? And it's light out. I'm confused."

What seemed like hours later, he finally saw the finish line. He raced towards it with the hardest effort of his life. After crossing it, tears of accomplishment cascaded down his cheeks. He next checked his watch. It read 4:17:30.

After accepting his finisher medal, Dylan approached him and wrapped him in a traditional post-race Scandinavian wool blanket. Mere seconds later, he was approached and then hugged by Uve, who had exclaimed to him with all the pride a fellow athlete can put forth, "Welcome to the club."

Good times... Mitch said to himself. *When Uve said that... Wow. That's the moment I finally considered myself a real runner.*

Thunder rumbled in the distance. It started to rain harder. Roo, in all her canine insanity, sought refuge from the booming in the distance by scuttling under the bed into a corner way too small for her seventy pounds, practically lifting the bed off the ground just to get to her refuge.

"That's good, Roo Roo!" said Dylan, recently woken from sleep, and now noticing Mitch's eyes wide open. "What's up?" she asked.

"I'm just thinking...Chicago, past marathons, CD's, the gigs, my training, exhaustion from having too much fun, perseverance, blah blah..." Mitch replied.

"Sweety, just go to sleep…" Dylan mumbled to herself in a voice similar to a soothing hypnotist. The word "sleep" seemed to put her right back into R.E.M.

With his first marathon experience thoroughly replayed in his memory's cinema and his confidence now boosted a few notches higher, his mind replayed his return home from Europe when he immediately wanted to sign up for the New York Marathon, the one race each runner he had spoken with in Norway had said was the greatest race experience ever. Mitch, however, had learned quickly that he wasn't the elite athlete or the really fast regular person he had needed to be in order to qualify for this world famous race; an athlete that wanted to run New York had to be really fast. In Mitch's eye, they had to be one of those super hero runners.

The Race Directors, however, took pity on slower amateurs like Mitch and regularly offered a lottery to win a trip to the starting line. Since the chances of winning a highly sought after lottery spot were slim to none, one aspect, which had helped to eclipse the frustration for runners like Mitch, was guaranteed entry to those applicants who had lost the lottery three years in a row.

Like clockwork, each year, Mitch had entered and gotten rejected. He had put a positive spin on each rejection knowing that he would finally get his chance to run in this great race in 2009. He embraced waiting for 2009 with the enthusiasm of a child waiting in a long and slow line for the best roller coaster in the world. He could be patient for a great thing.

To bide his time during his downtime between his Norway experience and racing in New York, he had decided to utilize his newly discovered passion for running marathons by entering a big city race which didn't require a qualifying time to get in. It was here, during DC's 2007 Marine Corps Marathon of twenty five thousand runners, where he had first experienced the footfalls of thousands of runners at the same time, the cheers of the huge crowds along the sidelines of the course, never being alone during a long race, and cherishing the deep and connecting bonds created by tired and weary runners late in the race.

I was working full time and gigging four times a week, but I trained smarter so I could break four hours in DC, he thought to himself as he became lost in the progression of how, after only running two marathons, he had become a competitive runner, but competitive only with himself and the digital mechanism he wore on his wrist.

His thoughts then meandered to the minutes after finishing DC, and how he couldn't wait to race in New York so he could set another personal record. *And I did!* he answered his thoughts. I slammed it with a 3:27. *I had the time to train right, and still do... I have no day gig. Run hard, nap, drive, gig.* He felt himself smile with the addition of nap to his daily routine.

I've definitely been bitten by the bug, he continued as his recent athletic past replayed itself out in chronologic detail while he stared into the emptiness of his bedroom. *But quitting my day job... That was it. I have time to train AND rest my body... That's a beautiful thing!* The runner paused in his thoughts and then added with a sense of unforeseen accomplishment, *My singing feeds my running.*

His active mind, now motivated to build up his confidence prior to a restful night's sleep, couldn't help but to recall how amazing of a summer and fall he had had in 2009, when he had trained for New York. His music schedule had seemed to simultaneously explode to up to seven or eight shows per week during this time. His voice's flowering brought him more and more offers to play shows. During some of his four-hour shows, his sets had grown to ninety, then to over one hundred minutes long; his running stamina had assisted with his ability to sing, similar to the way his training had helped him to persevere and run longer.

He then looked back to his success regarding his approach to how he had trained for New York. He had learned about speed workouts and how a focused hard and fast workout on the sandy horse track, located at the fairgrounds a few minutes from his home, could build up his strength to keep a faster and more consistent pace deep into his longer runs. *I wonder what people driving by must think when they see me racing around the track like a thoroughbred wanna-be,* the runner thought. *And when the horses in their harnesses pulling their riders in their chariots are sharing the track with me... That's a trip! I like imagining myself part horse.*

His thoughts then turned to his wife. Dylan had also blossomed in her athleticism during this time, becoming an incredibly accomplished runner and qualifier for the 2009 New York race, which she entered so she could run alongside Mitch. *She's amazing*, Mitch thought. *She races a half marathon, places second in her age group, and just like that, she's qualified and entered into a race I had to wait four years to get into... And she's so damned humble about her fitness... Like she's not doing anything great.*

As he lay there listening to the rain stopping and the trees dripping their monotonous drips through the canopy, he thought about that beautiful summer. When their timing had allowed, they had trained together. Their workouts had them both bathed in golden sunlight and sheltered from all negativity, regardless of what the reality had been like outside their athletic bubble. They had grown together. They had gotten faster together. They had loved even harder, though at this point in their relationship, they didn't think this was possible.

Though their race starting assignments for New York had them in two different starting corrals, they had run equally strong, finishing within minutes of each other. After the race's finish, the huge kiss, which had greeted their souls when they reconnected outside of Central Park was, to Mitch, bordering on the greatness of the kiss when they had sealed their marriage.

Their race had been consistent. Their times both had been under three hours and thirty minutes. Their goals had been met. Their love had been flowing strong. *Wow,* was all Mitch could say to himself as he stared at the opaque ceiling, now slightly illuminated by the waxing late rising moon as it subtlety broke through the departing storm clouds. *We took full advantage of life that amazing day and took nothing for granted.*

Feeling both love and gratitude, Mitch couldn't help but roll over and kiss his wife's cheek as the memories of last year's New York race brought out his love for Dylan from the deepest depths of his being. He smiled as Dylan's "I love you" response, spoken from a deep sleep, couldn't be any more real. It was nice.

All right, he thought. *So here I am… All elated as I think about how far I've come. So why am I so damned nervous to race Chicago in a few months?* He lay silently. A barred owl hooted in the distance. The reality of why he felt slightly out of sorts then hit him.

When I raced New York, I played a ton of shows, exhausted myself with fun, but still managed to run a great race. But I rested for the two weeks prior to the race. I barely played gigs in the few weeks leading up to it. I had shown up to the starting line as a well rested runner. His mind then spoke the truth to him as the consequence for his planning became obvious to him. *More than likely, I'm going be working my ass off up to the night before the start of Chicago… And I have no idea how the hell my body will react.*

After a few deep breaths, slightly nervous rationalization took over. *I'm training for it now, though… Run, drive, gig, repeat. I sing and I run. That's what I do. Everything will be great.*

Though it felt good to convince himself that he was where he needed to be, the nagging feeling that the pre-production, which he would need to complete in order to be efficient when it was time to go into the studio, had been eating into his rest time; the same rest time, which made training for New York so much fun, was now imposed upon, making training for Chicago more difficult.

He knew the up-front work in laying down the pre-production roughs for his new record were equally as important to the record's success as intervals and long runs were equally as important to the success of running a strong marathon. But there was only so much time in a day, and only so much stamina a music-athlete has.

To be working on my pre-pro when I should be running, to be running when I should be resting, to be resting when I should be singing, were the next thoughts to invade the athlete's mind. *What the heck? Not even thirty seconds ago, I was feeling good and building my confidence to the moon, but now all of a sudden, the rocket explodes?* he yelled at himself. *I'm not too manic,* he said sarcastically.

The runner took a deep breath. Soundless lightning lit up the room for a brief second as a second thunderstorm moved in and snuffed out the moon's soft light. The barred owl inquisitively hooted again from a different location.

Mitch mellowed. It seemed his brain flipped quicker than a line cook flipping fast-food burgers. He knew he was working hard and running just as hard. His shin hurt from running his training runs faster than he knew he should, simply so he could get that nap in before the night's upcoming show. His voice, though still full of song, was starting to show some wear from his multiple performances coupled with the hours of singing pre-production tracks into his home studio recorder.

Regardless of how difficult accomplishing both tasks might be, he knew, deep inside himself, that all his hard work would pay off and he'd sound great on his new CD and run a kick ass race. He didn't know how, but he'd make it work.

He was scared and confident, psyched and intimidated, and overwhelmed with the fortunate choices he made for himself. *If I weren't so afraid about what was coming up, I'd probably get too overconfident and screw everything up! It's all good. I've been here before. I've been tired before and pushed through with amazing results.*

I've blown my mind by what I can accomplish when the starting gun goes off or when I step into the studio to make a CD.

He paused and listened to his wife's deep breaths. *I got this,* was his next thought as his mind's late night optimism orgasmed and proceeded to finally slow, shut down, and embrace sleep.

Yes, to sleep. This was indeed his favorite part of the day.

The owl, now closer, once again hooted his repetitive question. To Mitch, the inquiry was further away as his eyes finally closed. When sleep overtook him that night, the runner couldn't help but think a final conscious thought: *I'm so fortunate to have my self-imposed demands be my primary problems… Tis a beautiful thing.*

As his breathing became more regular and dreams of randomness took away all of his cares, it was Roo who answered the owl's inquiry with soft dream squeaks, a by-product of her happy puppy dreams, envisioning running next to her daddy.

Tempo

T he overcast sky spread across the field from end to end. The summer temperatures were held in check by the cloud cover, though the temperature wasn't what was worrying Mitch. The vehicle's air conditioner pumped out dry and intoxicating coolness as the runner sat in the driver's seat. He stared out through the windshield at the eight hundred meter horse track and it's sandy oval. He knew that as soon as the engine was cut and the door was opened, the day's muggy and soupy environment would overtake him.

Do I really want to be running intervals today? Mitch asked himself. *I know the sun isn't going to beat me down, but to run four 800's in this eighty five degree mugginess…* The truck continued to idle. The runner took a deep breath and cursed himself for not listening to Dylan's suggestion to run early to beat the heat. "Oh Dylan, if you only knew how hard it is for me to wake early after getting home late from a show," he said to the air conditioner's power switch as he turned the knob to zero and twisted the ignition key of his truck to the off position. "Today is the only day this week for me to do these. Gotta do it," he said as he opened the truck's door and rolled his body out into the thick humidity.

He kicked off his flip flops, sat down on the grass, and put on his socks and shoes. For no reason he could discern, "Althea," by the Grateful Dead popped into his head. The lazy tempo of Jerry Garcia's guitar wooed him from his sitting position to standing.

"I told Althea, I was… feeling lost. Lacking in some direction," he sang to himself. Looking at the sand of the oval from where he was parked, he opened his truck door, grabbed his water bottle and put it on the roof. He took off his shirt, threw it inside the truck, shut the door, and lolly-gagged at Jerry's lazy pace towards the track.

"Can't talk to me, without talking to you, we're guilty of the same old thing..." Mitch sang as he dropped his water bottle by one of the track's well pumps and embraced a slow warm up trot. Sweat began to fall from his head as he completed the first turn of the oval. *Really?* he said to himself. *OK, note to self… Don't judge your speed by the times you post today. It's hot.*

"*Doh Doh Doh Doh, da Doh da Doh Doh Doh do Doh, mmm-Doh Doh,*" he sang aloud, mouthing Jerry's guitar brilliance. He let his warm up fall into the same slow tempo of this song. Though the mugginess surrounded him, the rhythm of the music in his head helped him to embrace the heat rather than fight it.

He came around the track to the starting point and decided that his body wasn't quite ready to push hard. He continued on around again, telling himself that a one mile warm up would be better for his body. Muscles now a little more fluid and his pace a little faster, "Althea" left his brain and was replaced by The Beatles', "Norwegian Wood," a recent addition to his solo acoustic set list. The runner involuntarily set his second warm up lap to the song's slightly faster waltz-like tempo.

"I once had a girl, or should I say, she once had me..." he sang as his pace picked up a bit and he hit the back stretch of the sandy track. "Doooo, do do do doooo, do do do doooo, do do do doooo." The song's instrumental led him around the track's final turn.

All right, he said to himself as the musical part of his mind continued with his soundtrack. *Mellow pace until my water bottle, and then kick it.* He was a few yards away from the starting point and reminded himself, *Sprint, but don't kill yourself.*

The runner hit the lap button on his stopwatch. He dug in his shoes on the soft sand. He gave it his all. His 'all' was slow. *I feel like I'm in a dream and running in place with a monster closing in on me!*

Approaching the first turn of the track, The Ramone's "I Wanna be Sedated," popped into his head. The fast tempo of this timeless punk-rock song resonated in his mind, traveled down his spine, and out towards the muscles in his legs. The feeling of not being able to run faster than a one-legged great grandma suddenly left him.

"Twenty twenty twenty four hours agohhhh, I wanna be sedated," rang through his mind as his legs matched the upbeat tempo of the song. Over the back stretch of the track, he held his pace - stride for stride - during the song's instrumental riffs. Approaching the third turn, he felt himself slow, but pushed himself to stay with the song. "Bah bah mm bah bah, mm bah bah mm bah bah, I wanna be sedated." *Stay with the song!* he yelled at himself. His legs complied.

He crossed the finish line and let his body drag. He walked. He looked down at his watch. *Wow, that tune is three minutes and ten seconds long... I think?* He knew that he wasn't singing the exact tempo of the song, but whatever was in his head had certainly pushed him to stay consistent.

Mitch turned back toward the start line. He bent for his water, took a swig, dropped it, and picked up a mellow jog in the opposite direction. Because of the heat, he didn't want to stay out too long. *I don't know... Maybe a ninety second rest interval before I start my second sprint?* He answered himself by pressing the lap button on his watch and slid into the minute and a half jog.

"Tonight, the Bottle Let Me Down," by Merle Haggard was the next random lazy tune to pop into his head. The hokey, old school country melody caused his body to bounce in ways similar to a stereotypical horse stumbling across the prairie in an old western movie. Haggard's cry that "I've always haaaaad a bottle, I could turn to..." helped his breathing return to normal.

The runner wiped some sweat from his forehead. The heat was certainly not comfortable for him, but it wasn't affecting him in the harsh way he had imagined while sitting in his truck. *Let's see what I feel like on the fourth interval,* the pessimistic side of his brain chimed in as Merle Haggard's twang thankfully drowned out his negativity. *Give it your all, but don't kill yourself,* he thought as he turned back towards the start line and commenced his forty five second count to the next sprint.

After all of the years on stage by himself or with different bands, Mitch had learned a bottomless amount of melodies and lyrics. Empowering this spontaneous mental jukebox, he wondered what the next song to pop into his head would be as he picked up his pace. As the start line quickly approached, he wondered, *Does every runner who doesn't run with headphones do this?*

He hit the lap button on his watch and waited for a song to enter his brain as his legs picked up their momentum. He tried to sing the Ramones again, but the heat prevented him from running as fast this time around. *Gimme something!* he yelled as he ran through the first turn.

The runner embraced his breathing. His hard working lungs caused the air he exhaled to exit his mouth with a staccato rhythm. *My breathing sounds like the drum groove to Bob Seger's "Hollywood Nights,"* he said to himself. A millisecond later, its upbeat groove filled his mind like a coliseum's sound system.

"She stood there bright as the sun on that California coast… He was a midwestern boy on his own," he sang as he sighted the sandy backstretch and it's two hundred and fifty meter straightaway. Again, he stayed with the song's tempo. He pushed. "And those Hollywood nights… And those Hollywood hills… Above all the lights… With its passion and thrills…" lyrics that had nothing to do with his workout, except to lend it a cadence and push him as he leaned forward across the finish line.

Two down, two to go… Holy shit. It is hot! He forced the upbeat song from his brain and replaced it with a mellower one, one which meant a lot to him. "I am just a poor boy though my story's seldom told… I have squandered my resistance, with a pocket full of mumbles such are promises." *I love what "The Boxer" does for my head… It always puts life into such a neat perspective*, he reminded himself as Paul Simon's lyrics sang away and paced him at a nice and slow resting jog.

Instead of running there and back to kill the time for his rest interval, he instead ran ahead of the starting line, turned around after twenty seconds, went back for his water, and chugged half the bottle. *Not too quick.* Cramps are not fun during hard workouts. He tossed the bottle aside, walked twenty feet behind the start line, and looked at his watch. He'd been resting for almost two minutes. *Time to motor*, and let the song's "Lye la Lye's" fade into the back of his mind.

Mitch picked up his jog, hit the start line, and pressed the lap button on his watch. Again, he felt like he was running in a pool of thick tar. As he rounded the first turn, he knew: *I need to push it, but if I push too hard, I'm gonna hurt myself… And that would suck. I need a fast tempo tune that isn't over the top… C'mon mind!* Rush's "The Spirit of Radio" popped into his head.

Running around the second turn and into the backstretch, he smiled at the up-tempo rhythm that his mind just offered him. "Begin the day with a friendly voice, a companion unobtrusive… Plays that song that's so elusive and the magic music makes your morning mood," sang Geddy Lee as Mitch's tempo matched Neil Peart's snare hits stride for stride.

Breathing a little easier with this for pacing instead of a punk anthem, he cruised around the track with the ease of the harness racers for which the track was designed. As the runner crossed the finish line and hit the lap button on his watch, he was psyched that the interval ended before the song's time and tempo change that most Rush songs from the late-seventies contained. *That would have thrown my pace for a loop*, he thought. *I can't even sing the crazy run that those guys do, much less match the pace with my legs!"*

As Mitch sipped a few gulps from his water bottle, he let the song's time change and final minute of the song play along in his head. "For the words of the prophets are written on the studio wall... Concert hall!" Mitch dropped his bottle and walked away from the starting line in the opposite direction. "Echoes with the sound, of salesmen... Of salesmen... Uuuuuuuv salesmen!" continued Geddy as Mitch caught himself playing air guitar and singing Alex Lifeson's guitar solo.

Thirty seconds later, the song ended. *One left*, Mitch said to himself. *Just one left... But I think the humidity level just kicked up a notch*, he said as he looked down at his soaked shorts. *One left*, was his answer to his fears of the heat.

The runner slowly jogged to the start line, crossed it, screamed "GO!" and hit his watch's lap button. He ran with a fury towards the first turn. A song he just learned, Foo Fighters "Everlong," hit him. His hard working legs gravitated towards the tune's fast chunking guitars as Dave Grohl sang, "Hello... I've waited here for you, everlong. Toooo-night, I throw myself intoooo, and out of the red, out of her head, she sang,"

Perfect, Mitch said to himself. *I'm dead on with the tempo. I just gotta hold it.* His running shoes seemed to kick up more sand with each stride. He felt the heat hit his brain as his vision became a little blurry. He pushed through it. *Last one... Push it! Give it your all!*

"If anything can ever be this real forever. If anything can ever be this good again. The only thing I ever ask of you, you gotta promise not to stop when I say when... She sang," screamed Dave Grohl as Mitch rounded the final corner and sprinted towards the finish. *Don't fall off pace... You got this!* yelled the runner to himself. *Thirty seconds and you're done running... Hold on!*

Moments later, he crossed the finish line. Mitch let his legs buckle as he dropped to a knee. His elevated breathing continued as he took his right hand, crossed it over his chest, and patted himself on his left shoulder. "Good job," he said aloud and stood up.

The runner walked to his water bottle, picked it up, chugged it, refilled it from the well, and chugged the whole thing. He knew that he should commence a cool down lap so he wouldn't cramp up, but he thought better of it since the heat and humidity suddenly began to overwhelm him.

Still breathing hard, he let Jerry Garcia's calming riff from "Althea" come back to him. He took a few more deep breaths and finally regulated his breathing. *OK, no more running, but maybe a walk around the track to keep me loose.* Inevitably, halfway through the walk, he began to jog to Jerry's tempo.

Five minutes later, back in his truck with his air conditioner cranking, he thought about what he had just accomplished. It was always difficult for him to get out and do a hard workout alone, especially in the heat. But for a singer who works most nights and only has the time to run when the rest of the world is working, it was a sacrifice he'd gladly make for his music.

As he pulled away from the track and headed back home, he thought about how close he had come to blowing off the workout. He then smiled as he thought about one of his favorite running mantras: You might not regret the run that you blow off, but you'll never regret the run that you do.

6

Thirty Six Hours

The Mahogany, which hung in old school Victorian Irish design throughout the lively tavern, reflected the harsh glow of the incandescent lamps. Just recently dimmed and warm, they were now a voiceless, bright, and uninviting message to the pub's late night patrons: Closing time. The singer spoke into his microphone one last time that evening and offered his heartfelt thanks to all those he and his band had just connected with. He looked left, caught his fellow players' eyes, and took delight in how much fun they had just had.

Neil and Drew had been playing with Mitch for almost ten years. Over and over, throughout their continued time together on stage, when the vibe of the room was right, when the sound of the band was dialed into the room's acoustics perfectly, and when they were *on*, for the three of them, it never got old.

As Neil packed his sticks into his stick bag and Drew switched off his bass amp, all Mitch could think to do was to sit, take a few deep breaths, and decompress.

"How are you holding up, Mitch?" asked Drew.

"You know, even with singing two gigs around all of the driving, I feel amazing!" Mitch answered. "I kind of feel like I do after finishing a strong twenty mile training run." He thought for a second and concluded, "I'm tired, but in an energized and amazing way!" After looking down at his second soaked shirt of the day, he placed his butt on the edge of the stage and dangled his legs over the lip in a way similar to an idle marionette puppet's restful perch. The singer took a deep breath, wiped his brow, and was psyched and grateful to thank the folks who went out of their way to walk past him to wish him a good night and a thumbs up for the band's sound.

After the majority of the crowd filed past him on their way to embrace the warm and salt scented air of the summer night, which was generously offered by the northern New England coast, Mitch looked at both Neil and Drew and said, "That was awesome! Man, the band's sound is constantly growing." He nodded his head and added, "I love how each gig kicks it up another notch."

"No doubt," Drew responded.

"Good vibe," Neil added. "Hot. Sweaty. Summertime. High energy. Kick ass!"

The singer thought about how he had spent his time prior to meeting his band and said, "I had a great solo show on The Brunswick's patio today, but during the drive up to Portland, all I kept thinking was "But tonight, I get to rock." And then we did. What fun!"

Mitch swung his dangling legs forward and back as he excitedly embraced life. *I love how it all just feels so right. Being a band rocking in the local bars instead of striving for the major label deal and putting my happiness in the hands of corporate music...* "So good!" he said aloud.

A moment later, the bar manager approached the stage holding three full pints in a triangle formation between his clutched spidery fingers. "Hell of a night!" boasted Evan, spoken with the accent of a native farmer from Dublin, coupled with a smile that could put Santa Claus on Christmas Eve to shame. The bartender placed a cold glass in each band member's hands and shook hands with each of them. "Always a pleasure, fellahs!" he said and turned to the backs of the leaving crowd and added his voice to the chanting bouncers, "Everybody out! Finish 'em up! Everybody Out!"

Hearing the bouncers verbally whip the leaving patrons, Drew offered his opinion on what they were witnessing. "The bar scene can be so silly sometimes."

"Sometimes?" Neil questioned rhetorically as his cymbals disappeared into their case.

Resonating throughout the pub were screeching sounds on the wood floors, which were made by the fast moving bar-backs as they manipulated the tables back into place for the restaurant's morning brunch. Coupled with these noises were the clangs of the many empty pint glasses being collected by the wait staff.

"They don't waste any time," Neil said and rose from behind his kit. He locked Mitch's eyes for a moment and then looked at Drew. He raised one hand over his head, palm out, and said, "Great show!" Drew high-fived Neil as Mitch, still dangling his legs over the stage, laid his back onto the stage and outstretched his arm over his head in order to receive Drew's other congratulatory palm. Each expressed their agreement that it had been a golden gig.

Mitch stopped sweating. He could feel his body cooling down nicely. It felt good. After a few sips of his newly acquired beverage were in his belly, he kicked his legs back onto the stage, rose from his Humpty Dumpty-like viewpoint, and got into his post-gig mode.

First things first, Mitch said to himself as he pulled down all the PA channel faders except for the one that controlled the small stage monitor; he loved spinning mellow tunes at low volumes through the compact speaker at the end of a high-energy night. To him, great music played at low volumes after a high energy rock show mimicked the blissful feeling of the one to two mile cool down run after a hard run.

For Mitch, after such a fulfilling show, tonight's decompression tunes were hardly disputed. He quickly shuffled through the Ipod's menu, found what he was looking for, hit the play button, and adjusted the volume to what he considered mellow talking volume. Bob Weir voiced through the stage monitor, "Now we're gonna play everybody's fun game, 'Take a Step Back.'"

"You guys cool with Cornell, '77?" Mitch asked his friends.

"I couldn't agree more," said Neil. Drew smiled and nodded.

Bass and guitars now in their cases and all the plugs disconnected from their relevant connections, the seemingly endless winding of cables commenced as the three musicians sang along to "Scarlet Begonias." There was a rhythm to this part of the night and the efficiency it required to both break down a rock club PA and be packed up and out of a club within an hour. Mitch placed the cable crates in the middle of the stage for their easy collection after coiling. Drew took the speakers off their stands and consolidated them with guitar and bass amplifiers by the pub's exit while Neil broke down his drums and the hardware which held them in place.

Ten minutes into the band's breakdown, Evan again approached the stage and handed the band's bar tab and the night's earnings to Mitch. Mitch pocketed the check and paid Evan for the bar tab with the cash from the tip jar that housed the night's CD sales. They thanked each other, smiled, and shared an earnest handshake.

The three worked hard while chatting amongst themselves. They had their routine dialed in. Though it seemed like a lot of work, especially after putting so much energy into their show, they loved what they did. To each of them, it was all just part of the bliss of being in a local band rocking in a local bar.

"I'm psyched to record some more music with you guys," Mitch said.

Neil responded as he placed his drums in their cases. "I know you want this next CD to have a solo record vibe to it, so I'm wondering about the three tracks I'll be on?"

"Hit them in time," said a sarcastic Drew, his voice projected away from them as he carried one of the speakers towards the door.

Mitch laughed. "Drew..." he said in a low voice and then directed his voice towards Neil. "Focused and tight while imagining playing to tonight's crowd," Mitch replied. "I might be making a solo record, but the songs that rock, I want to really rock."

Speaker staged by the door, Drew turned back towards his friends and remarked, "Play the songs better than a normal drummer."

Again, Mitch laughed, this time joined by both Neil and Drew. The three then collectively reminisced about the person who, several years ago, had approached them while they were enjoying their 2AM post-gig early breakfast pit stop in Bangor on their way back to Portland.

Neil put on his best northern Maine accent and said, "You were the band playing at The Waterfront tonight! You guys rocked! Wicked good! Much better than a normal band."

Mitch followed up the impersonation by asking the two of them, "Was I really that rude when I asked, 'What's a normal band?'"

"Not at all," said Drew. "He was wasted... What was so funny was that his answer was, 'Well, ummm... You didn't play "Mustang Sally" or "Freebird." You know.. Better than a normal band.'"

The musicians continued to work and chat. Mitch found the tasks he assigned himself to be very relaxing and thanked the pub for kicking everyone out at exactly 1AM. In some bars, after the band finished, folks were allowed to stay around as long as they weren't drinking. This would inevitably lead to one or two moderately inebriated people standing in the middle of the stage, clueless that the band needed to break their gear down, trying their best to engage in random conversation with any band member willing to listen.

"I love music fans and totally appreciate that they like seeing us, but it's really funny what they talk about after the gig, when they're hammered," said Neil.

"The best was definitely the horseradish guy," Drew answered.

"I don't even remember what he was babbling about for the twenty minutes before the horseradish comment." Neil said. "All I remember is trying not to pee in my pants from laughing so hard!"

Mitch couldn't hold back his smile as he remembered that moment. "It seems that I'm always the perceived rude one when very drunk people start talking to me. Am I really that much of an ass to them during breakdown?"

Drew answered through his own laughter and said, "No, you're just honest. Those people don't think you're an ass. It just seems like you're rude because they're hammered and you're making them think... And hammered people don't like to think."

"How long did he talk to you guys before coming over to me?" Mitch asked.

"At least ten minutes to each of us," answered Neil. "I was so happy when he finally got out of my way so I could get my stuff packed up and then couldn't do anything but listen to your conversation with him since it was so funny."

It was Drew who then put on his 'downeast Maine' accent as he wound cables and impersonated the horseradish guy. "Fast acoustic guitar strumming is wicked awesome! Chrize, you're good at that. But I like playing a mandolin. I like to strum my mandolin fast, Bub. And I strum really fast when I play it all distorted-like through my guitahh amp. And wicked loud!"

Mitch then interjected, "All I was doing was asking the guy if he knew "Leftover Salmon." I mean, if you're a mandolin player and play your instrument cranked through a Marshall stack, chances are you know them… It's what "Leftover Salmon" is known for."

"Yeah, but the look on his face when you asked him if he liked that band," said Neil. "The way his eyes crossed while he was thinking… That was hilarious!"

"For most of our breakdown, all he was talking about was music," said Drew. "And then you go and ask him if he likes "Leftover Salmon," and he straightens up, crosses his eyes, thinks about it for ten seconds, accepts that you're changing the conversation to food, leans in towards you, and says with a slurred drunken stupor, 'Well, yeah… But with a little horseradish.'"

The three were now collectively cracking up. Neil said through his laughter, "When you said 'No, man… The band "Leftover Salmon,"' it totally screwed with his mind. He didn't know what to talk about afterward and finally left us to break down. Too funny."

As the story reached it's close and the band members reminisced of other late night silliness, the final cables needed to be coiled and the heavier gear needed to be stacked by the door. Unfortunately for the three of them, appreciative listeners of a good vintage Grateful Dead show, this occurred while Jerry was tickling each of them with his "Fire on the Mountain" solo.

"Sorry guys," said Mitch. He eased the monitor's fader down to zero and turned off the Ipod.

Breakdown almost complete, the singer thought to himself how, after such a satisfying gig, it was great to be able to pack up their gear while listening to a timeless band do their thing. This inspired him to change the conversation's direction back to their music and to speak to his band mates about next month's studio session.

"I cannot wait to go into the studio with you guys!" he said.

"You already said that," responded Drew, "But it's gonna be such a blast that it bears repeating."

"It does!" said Mitch.

Drew continued, "But we need to do it right, even if Neil and I are only playing on three of the tunes."

"Agreed," Mitch said. "When we go in, we need to capture the same good energy we put out here tonight. If we can do that, the productions of the songs you guys play on will effortlessly fall into place."

"What about the other five tunes?" asked Neil. "I'm concerned it'll sound disjointed, recording three rock tunes here and then you recording five acoustic tunes later on in Chicago."

"I'm thinking we'll feel out what that moment in time brings and run with it then," answered Mitch. "But getting the first three tunes down with you guys will only help my approach to the others. My gut tells me that if we nail the three rock tunes next month, it's only going to inspire me when I get to Matt's to record the other five acoustic tunes. It's going to be a super fun process," he said with a smile as the final pieces of gear were packed away and staged by the door. "Thanks again for being a part of it," he finished.

As soon as this last statement left his lips, Mitch felt his belly rumble. His thought process involuntarily fell in line with his time management lifestyle. Changing the subject, he said, "It's 1:40. If we're gonna get food, we need to get to Otto's by two. The truck is parked a half mile away and still needs to be packed. I'm gonna motivate." Just like that, without asking any questions, giving any direction, or stating the obvious, the athlete was out the door and running an eight hundred meter interval at a 6:45 pace. Minutes later, the truck was parked on the sidewalk outside the bar's front door with Mitch on his knees inside the capped pickup's bed calling out the gear which needed to be loaded first.

Loading a full PA system and stage gear into the back of a mid-sized pickup truck can be very akin to the video game Tetris, where all the pieces need to fit tight, secure, and even. Over the several years of participating in this real life puzzle, coupled with the silliness caused by lifting heavy gear late at night after rocking a high energy show, each piece of equipment took on a name of its own: 'Sub-a-Dub' for the subwoofer, 'Gerbil' for each JBL speaker, 'Kick-Bass' and 'Floordom' for the larger drums, 'Kick Ass Prosonic' for the Fender guitar amp, 'So-crates' for the cable crates, pronounced the same way as in the movie "Bill and Ted's Excellent Adventure," and finally, Mitch's favorite, the 'Purple Monkey Bass Amp.'

Drew's bass cabinet, which had been custom built by a good friend and delivered to him unfinished, got its name's inspiration from his daughter who had insisted he spray paint the speaker cabinet purple. Several days later, Mitch had seen an episode of "The Simpson's" where an assembled crowd had played an impromptu game of Telephone; a rumor was whispered through a crowd of hundreds of people and somehow the term "purple monkey dishwasher" got tagged onto the end of the initial statement. Mitch had thought this was brilliant. During the next gig's breakdown, he had repeated, through his own laughter, the animated scene to Neil and Drew. Later, as they were packing the truck and Mitch had called for Drew's speaker cabinet, Drew hoisted it up into the back of the truck and said to Mitch, "Here's the purple monkey bass amp." The name stuck.

Tetris game completed and their work done for the night, Mitch said, "All right, one quick idiot check and it's pizza time! You guys take the Jeep... I'll meet you there." The singer ran into the bar and gave a quick glance around the empty stage area. Satisfied that his forgetful mind saw nothing left behind, he shouted out a "goodnight" to the employees still cleaning up, jumped behind his truck's steering wheel, and met up with Drew and Neil, who were standing in the short line outside of the pizza place. "Yes!" he said to them as he joined them on line. "Five minutes to spare."

Pizza on plates in front of them, the band let themselves absorb the ecstasy of Otto's pizza as they sat outside at a table on the restaurant's frontage and finally relaxed; the physical tension in their muscles seemed to slip away with each bite in a way similar to a marathoner diving into a huge recovery cheeseburger after running a hard race. Eating more and talking less, interspersed with their chewing, swallowing, and "mmm's," each player recounted their high points of the night's show and offered their opinions on the flow of the improvised set list, the experimental tones of their instruments, and the collective energy and live connections they had with each other. It felt great.

Sustenance achieved, Mitch was the first to rise. He hugged Drew and Neil, further complimented each of them on a great performance, and jumped back into his truck. He was psyched that tonight he was staying in Portland and didn't have to make the hour long late night drive back to his home in the foothills.

Instead, the runner's cross town commute to Janet and Paul's place was only seven minutes. As he drove, he thought of Dylan sleeping in the guest room with five hours of good sleep likely already under her belt.

In a few hours, she would wake, meet Janet and Paul in the kitchen, and help brew up the morning's coffee in preparation for the 10K they would all be participating in, just three hours from their first sip.

Mitch let his mind wander as he played out the rhythm of the following morning in his head. He imagined the three of them pinning their numbers on their shirts, putting their timing chips on their shoes, stretching, and welcoming with enthusiasm and nervousness the rising of the sun and the anticipation of the day's race.

He then envisioned that after two cups of coffee, Dylan would ease back into the room where she and Mitch had slept. She would wake him as slowly and tenderly as only she knew how. She'd give him a cup of coffee and then hand him his race gear. When the fuzziness of the night's three to four hours of limited rest would finally recede to the edge of his ears, the athlete would then dress, wash his face with cold water, look in the mirror, laugh at the puffiness in his eyes, smile again while thinking of the previous night's show, brush his teeth, and would then join his fellow running friends downstairs in the kitchen.

He imagined that by the time he would make it downstairs, Kathy, Ellie, Sarah, Al, Chuck, Tom, and Amy would all be there chatting about family, training, projected finish times, and arranging carpools to and from the race. When Mitch would enter the kitchen, he would expect them each to laugh at the sleepy look on his face while congratulating him on his motivation to race the day's distance on almost no sleep and after such a late night.

He thought about how the clock would eventually push the runners out the door and towards the starting area where a huge field of five thousand runners would be congregated. At this time, akin to a caterpillar which has just shed his skin to become a butterfly, he knew that the sleepy, fuzzy feelings would dissipate from his mind and would leave in their wake a motivated music-athlete.

He envisioned himself warming up with everyone, pointing his mind's drive on a PR, and running his heart out at the fastest tempo 10K his fitness would allow. He would celebrate at the finish, go out for post race beers and burgers with his wife and friends, and would eventually head home and take a huge power nap before the following night' show.

I have a really fun day planned for tomorrow! Mitch said to himself as he pulled into Janet and Paul's driveway. A random introspective feeling made him wonder how long he could keep up with such a nutty schedule. *I'll just keep doing my thing as long as my body allows… And enjoy each day I get to be me.*

Truck locked and gear secure, he made his way into the house using the hidden spare key and, as expected, found Dylan fast asleep in the guest room. As he climbed into bed next to her, he again thanked the Universe for such a fortunate life.

I hope I can break forty three minutes tomorrow was his last thought as his mind entered insta-R.E.M.

~~~~~~~~~~~~~~~

2:17 AM - I leave the guys at Otto's.

2:21 - I pass a cop who has pulled an unfortunate person over. I'm so glad I'm driving to Janet and Paul's and don't have to run the gauntlet through Gorham.

2:25 - I shut the truck's engine off. I grab my Martin and my Tele… Always take the guitars inside.

2:27 - I invade Janet and Paul's fridge for a Gatorade… It's silly that I'm just now getting into pre-race mode.

2:38 - It's hard to wind down from the gig and sleep. I nudge Dylan when her teeth start grinding. She stops, acknowledges, and doesn't even wake up. Man, I wish I could sleep as soundly as her!

6:03 - Dylan wakes me.

6:10 - I finally get out of bed. It's difficult, but I tell myself *running races on no sleep is what I do.* I ask myself *Why?* I tell myself to shut up and deal.

6:20 - I put my running uniform on and head to the bathroom. I splash cold water on my face because I think it's a good idea. It sucks. I turn on the hot water faucet, wait a few seconds, and bathe my face in the nurturing warmth. I stumble to the stairs and head down.

6:25 - I hug ten runners… Who are also great friends. It's really neat to see all of them.

6:26 - Ohhhh, coffee!

6:30 - I'm in the back seat of Janet's car alongside Dylan and Ellie. Gatorade hydration is my focus.

6:40 - We're in Al's driveway picking him up on the way to the race. It's a perfect time to stretch my hamstrings on the car's hood. I'm waking slowly... But I'm still really tired. Temps are nice. Stay nice, please.

6:50 - We pull into the large grassy field. I'm so thankful that I'm not driving as there are thousands of people and hundreds of cars. It's pre-race chaos.

7:00 - I'm in line at the porta potties... There must be over 100 of them! Doors are slamming. People are chatting. Music is playing over the tinny speakers temporarily mounted on the telephone poles.

7:07 - I leave the field with Dylan and walk to Route 77 and the race's start. People are everywhere!

7:10 - We take in the starting area and where we see ourselves when the horn goes off. We turn and swim against the current of people who are walking towards us to do the same.

7:12 - We meet up with Janet, Ellie, and Sarah and start warming up. We jog ten minutes away from the starting area, turn around, and jog back. Sleepiness is falling away.

7:32 - I wait in line at another porta-pottie. Thousands of others do the same.

7:38 - I visit an aid station, drink some water, and then meet back up with Dylan. We lock eyes, kiss, and get our race faces on. We walk towards the starting area. I'm fully awake now!

7:45 - We nudge ourselves through the masses and take our places just in front of the banner that says "7:00 pace."

7:48 - I jump over the waist high fence in the starting area, run into the woods, and relieve myself one last time. About a hundred other women and men are scattered a tenth of a mile back doing the same. We're all laughing at each other.

7:50 - The National Anthem is sung.

7:55 - We're all nerves and jitters while listening to the announcements and waiting for the race to start. The temperature is starting to rise. The humidity is getting thicker. I can smell the ocean now.

8:00 - The Wheelchair division starts. Five thousand runners are applauding.

8:03 - I kiss Dylan one last time before the horn goes off.

8:05 - We run!

8:12 - First mile, 6:30 pace… Too fast! Slow it! Save it for the end.

8:19 - Second mile, Gatorade gulp at the aid station. I look at my watch… I'm slightly slower. Good!

8:20 - I lose Dylan. She's dropped behind me. How can a tired Mitch be in front of a superhero like her? I go with it, embrace my body, and don't ask any more questions. I'll see her soon enough.

8:26 - I'm halfway… I've just run a 5K in a little over twenty minutes. I'm right on track with where I want to be.

8:27 - I skirt to the side of the course and run through a resident's spraying garden hose, which he has titled "The Shower of Power."

8:28 - We're on the main junction of roads in Cape Elizabeth. It looks like there are a thousand spectators. Music is playing. Cowbells are clanging. The fire department has their ladder trucks out and in full extension with a huge American Flag hanging from the top. The vibe is amazingly happy and filled with the energy of fast moving runners. We each do our best to smile as we pass the people cheering at the tops of their lungs, yet we're each experiencing the pain of pushing our bodies way past our comfort zones.

8:31 - I'm pushing myself harder. It hurts, but I don't want to let myself down.

8:32 - The course leads us down Shore Road. Millionaire's mansions dot the tree-lined street. I catch brief glimpses of the ocean in between the homes. The hills are minutes away. I'm getting tired. Last night's show is starting to weigh on my body. I'm still on pace, though. I keep running hard.

8:38 - I hit the mile five aid station. There's a silly sign that says, "It's no jive, you've hit mile 5." I'm not laughing. I'm hurting. All the runners around me are hurting. We're all pushing hard. We're all kicking ass. I look for Dylan. She's gotta be close to me.

8:39 - I'm on the hills. Runners are grunting around me. Some start walking. We're each running around a seven minute pace. It's hot. The entrance to the park is ahead. I hear the crowds. I'm almost done! This hurts. But it's great! I don't know why… It just is. We're runners running as fast as we can… Just because. We're each doing our best to keep each other psyched about our pace. "You got this!" is uttered from the mouths of fellow runners, spoken to their hurting brethren.

8:44 - I'm done with the hills. I'm in the park now and on the perimeter road. The crowds are deafening. The road is gated off so the crowds don't infringe on the runners. The path is only ten feet wide. Runners are doing their best to sprint to the finish.

8:45 - I hit the mile six marker. I don't know how much faster I can run. I'm passed by several runners who did the smart thing early on… They didn't go out too fast. I mentally yell at them as they breeze by me. *You didn't play two gigs yesterday and get into bed at 2:30AM last night!* This doesn't make me run faster.

8:46 - I round the last curve. The lighthouse is in front of me. The ocean is so immense I imagine I can see England. I view the finish line. I kick it as hard as I can. If I fall down at the end, whatever… I'm gonna finish this thing hard. I'm a runner!

8:46:07 - I finish. I ran a personal best. Holy shit. I'm dead… I do my best not to fall over. Did I really just hit a PR? I'm handed some water. The volunteer tells me and the other runners to keep moving away from the finish area. A medic asks me if I'm OK. I nod and keep moving forward. I grab a second water bottle from another volunteer in case Dylan misses the initial water-giving volunteers. I move to the side. I wait for Dylan. It's getting hotter. I feel bad for the folks running a ten minute per mile pace. *Just keep moving forward,* I mentally tell them.

8:47 - Dylan flies through the finish chute. I'm there to greet her. She also ran a PR. We're elated. We're so hot, but we kiss anyway. We smile. We kiss again. We hug.

8:50 - We're up at the lighthouse awaiting our friends. We're standing in the shade by one of the trailers that brought the complimentary food for the finishers.

9:01 - We meet up with our friends at the Results area. We each confirm our times and high five each other. My body is slowing down. I'm getting more and more tired with each passing minute.

9:15 - We're on a full school bus heading back to the start area to pick up our car. I'm laughing and shaking my head simultaneously as I look out the window and witness other runners who have decided to run back to the starting area instead of taking a bus. I'm perplexed at how athletic folks can train themselves to be... To race a 10K and then cool down with a six mile run? Amazing. Once I race, running is done for the day. I couldn't do what those folks are doing if I tried. I'm in awe of their fitness.

9:45 - We're back at Janet and Paul's place. I'm first to shower. Oh my... Bliss is an understatement!

10:15 - We're at the Dry Dock. We're on a third floor deck overlooking Portland Harbor at a table of fourteen. Each setting has a bloody mary in front of it. Each bloody mary is garnished with a salad and a shrimp. We're indulging. We're laughing. We're strategizing about the next race. I order a bacon cheeseburger for breakfast. I wake more and more with each liquid calorie ingested.

10:27 - We get our food. It's the best burger I've ever eaten!

11:30 - We say our goodbyes. Dylan jumps in her car, I jump in my truck. We drive the hour long ride home. Food coma is setting in. Tiredness is setting in. I'm getting so excited to nap.

12:45 - I'm in bed, my shades are drawn, I'm breathing deeply. I'm elated. My training is working. I just ran a 41:07 10K. According to professional running coaches in running magazines, I'm right on track to PR in Chicago.

2:50 - I wake… I look at the clock with wonder and amazement that I had just slept so long. I do some calculations. Two hours until I have to leave for the next gig… Perfect! Upon hearing the bed creak, Dylan enters the room and jumps into bed with me. She kisses me. We talk about how great it was to race and PR this morning. She then tells me how much fun she's had playing in the garden while I was recharging my internal batteries.

3:30 - I'm on my back deck. I'm drinking coffee and having a freshly picked salad for lunch while I bask in the late afternoon sunshine. Life feels so fantastic. I'm mellow, yet psyched about everything. With each passing minute, I'm effortlessly building momentum for tonight's show on "Jimmy's" patio.

5:00 - It's time to make beautiful music.

5:10 - Nothing on the radio… And I'm sick of the CD's I never get around to swapping out. I drive in silence.

5:17 - I do my five-minute vocal warm up. I've sang the same "La-Ga-Ya-Ga" warm ups before every show for the past fifteen years. They've never let me down. But each time I hear myself sing them, they always sound really dumb. I keep singing them.

5:30 - I arrive at the gig. The patio is empty. The stone is radiating heat. I load my gear to the stage area. I start to sweat my ass off. I'm glad I have on a beater shirt for the work part and a gig shirt in my bag for the performance part. I drink water from the quart sized bottle which I've brought along with me.

5:55 - Gear is set up. My shirt is changed. Temps are going down with the setting sun. Folks are starting to meander onto the patio. I have some set break music spinning on the Ipod over my PA. I'm hoping the vibe of my mix keeps them out here and psyched for me to start playing. I head inside to the blissful air conditioned bar to order a beer for my first set.

6:00 - I rock.

7:45 - *What fun! Thanks so much for hanging out, you guys!* I tell the large crowd. *It's time for me to take a break and so I can say "Hi" to y'all… I have a lot more music to sing so please stay around,* are my last words spoken into the mic just before hitting the play button on the Ipod. Set break time!

10:15 - Jimmy approaches the stage and thanks me for the show. I thank him for the work and we chat about business and the fun of summer.

10:34 - My truck is loaded and it's time to head home.

10:40 - I'm at a convenience store looking at the tall thermoses of really old coffee. I need some 'awake' help as yesterday's two gigs and lack of sleep before running this morning's PR and then singing tonight have me feeling more tired than usual. The afternoon's nap was great, but naps can only take me so far. I still hate bad coffee. I opt for bottled apple juice and a bag of chips instead. *It's only a half hour drive,* I tell myself.

11:15 - I head up Norton Road. I love driving up this hill. I love living on a mountain's side. The moon is beautiful as I crest over the road's highest point. Its light reflects off the distant trees and illuminates the starry sky beyond. *Every day… Every day…* I speak my mantra internally as I make myself instantaneously remember and forget my worst living conditions and thank the Universe for where I'm living now.

11:17 - I'm parked in my driveway. My truck's front door is open. Roo has her two front paws in my lap. Her nose is buried in my tummy. Her tail is wagging voraciously. I laugh, pet her, and hug her at the same time.

11:18 - I grab my Martin… Always grab the guitars.

11:30 - I share my toast with Roo. Dylan doesn't know I do this... She'd be angry with me, but I know she'd find the cuteness in it.

11:55 - I'm showered and comfortably horizontal. I won't sleep for a bit, but I'm OK with it. So much has happened over the last thirty six hours. My mind chronologically recants yesterday's solo show, last night's "Now Is Now" gig, this morning's race, and tonight's solo show. I'm feeling fortunate. I turn to a sleeping Dylan and kiss her cheek. I couldn't do what I'm doing without her support. This makes me feel even more fortunate.

12:12 - I tell myself that I'm not going to look at the clock again. I have tomorrow off. I'm so psyched to relax. My marathon training plan has me running five, but I've decided to blow it off and instead sit in a cool river. I rationalize that my schedule doesn't tell me to race a 10K PR the day before running the scheduled five. I internally giggle at my motivation to be lazy. I tell myself to shut up and to not take for granted the fitness which I've developed for myself. I take some deep breaths.

- Sleep... Deep sleep...

Ruff

T he waning August sun passed its peak in the sky, golden
rays of light pierced the forest canopy in crystalline strands.
Seasons are changing, thought the eleven-year-old shepherd/
husky mix who sat attentively in her dirt nest underneath the
crabapple tree in the front yard of her home. With most of
her winter coat gone, the cool breeze tickled her senses as the
aromas from the flowering vegetable garden floated by her long
and sensitive snout. It was a great day to be a doggy.

There was a faint stirring the house. It caused the animal to
leave her nest and get a better look and feel of things. She paced
with a tuned interest, part curiosity, part happiness, and part
knowing. *That sounds like a leash jingling... I know it! Umm... I bet
I'm going for a run with daddy... Oh boy! Try to be mellow... I know
I'm supposed to keep my excitement under control, but who wants to
control their excitement when you're about to run? No one... But it could
be anything... No... I know that sound... I'm going for a run!* The
dog's mind raced with the anticipation of unbridled happiness.

Roo might as well have had a circus horse's costume on.
She trotted proudly and happily around the perimeter of the
house while awaiting Mitch's inevitable exit from the basement.
Minutes later, the door clicked open and the runner emerged.

At seeing Mitch holding her leash in hand, Roo attempted a super excited yet incomplete back flip. *I knew it!* She approached him quickly, sniffed his shorts, recognized the smell, sat down, laid her ears back, opened her mouth, and started to pant lightly. She let a doggy smile take over her face and waited for the click of the leash, which attached her to the waist of one of her best friends. *We're going running!* Mitch smiled and laughed back at her knowing full well how much she lived for these moments.

It had been a few weeks since they hit the roads and trails together. The summer's unseasonably hot and humid weather combined with Mitch's inability to wake early before the temperatures climbed too high, delegated Roo to sit out much of the previous week's excursions; there's only so much exercise a dog who is bred for winter athletics can tolerate during peak heat season. This made today that much more special for her. Leash in place around Mitch's waist, latch firmly clipped into her collar, she made her friend heal at her side and led them down the driveway to explore her favorite four point two mile patrol.

They made a left at the driveway's base and continued down the opposite side of the mountain they would have to run up at the end of their chosen loop. Leash taught at his beltline, Mitch let the bouncing dog pull him downhill at an energized pace. The runner couldn't contain his laughter.

I know what you're thinking, Daddy, Roo said to herself as she listened to him babble about how starting slow and saving energy for the hill at the end of the run is important. *How many times do you say the same thing to me when we run out of the driveway? You know I can't obey* that *command.* Her mouth opened, her tongue stuck out about 2 inches, and her gate lengthened. *I have no idea how far I'm running... Two miles... Five miles... Ten miles. I don't care. I'm running... Nuff said!* She licked her jowls, opened her mouth back up, and continued her pant. *Each time we start our journey together, for those first few steps, it's run like hell!. That's just what I do. I can't help it.*

Mitch picked up his two legged pace in order to keep up with Roo's four legged tempo. Except for the clicking of Roo's paws and Mitch's footfalls on the dirt road, they ran in silence, taking in the sights and smells of the wilderness around them. When the dirt road dead-ended, they turned right down the mile long dormant snowmobile trail, past the Pease Farm with its grazing donkeys, and towards the right-hand turn that would bring them onto the paved main road.

C'mon Dad! Faster! Roo implied. *Look at me! Look at you! This is what life is about! I love this so much. I don't care that you're pulling me back. You pull, I run harder... That's the rule.* Roo looked at Mitch and gave him a wide a doggy smile. *We should just run as fast as we can. Don't you think? Wait... STOP! This smells lovely.*

Mitch almost fell face first onto the dirt as Roo's sudden desire to indulge on the champagne smells of the earth put her now motionless body directly in front of his energized cadence; the pebbles on the dirt road's surface provided the perfect terrain for him to come to a sliding stop just before the still and perpendicular dog. Roo smelled around for a few seconds, took care of her business, looked up at Mitch, turned her body, and again bolted ahead, pulling her daddy behind her.

A half mile later, the two exited from the trail, made a right turn, and pranced down the main road. With more purchase now underneath her paws, Roo picked up the pace even more. *This is where I get to show off my running to the other dogs.* She said to herself. *Soon we'll pass the beagles in their pen, the barking boxers at their living room window, and the poodle who's always screaming from his bedroom window.* Roo cantered in her proudness as she thought about how all the other dogs wanted to be like her, to be a runner.

Another mile down the road, Roo's ears went from flat to erect and alert. Simultaneously, Mitch pulled their pace back a little. *In just a minute, we'll be at the crazy striped dog's house. I don't know why, but he always wants to eat my Daddy… Even though he never did anything to him.* She thought about this for a few seconds and then added, *But I hold the title. That's what my Daddy says. I'm The Champion Fighting Queen.* Roo licked her lips as she answered Mitch's tug with one of her own. She became excited about staring down the striped dog, one on one. *No one eats my Daddy.*

As they approached the house of the striped dog, from out of the woods adjacent to the house came the barking menace. With his teeth barred and hackles up, he ran across the two lane highway with high hopes of eating a dog and a human for lunch. Mitch turned, raised and lowered his arms like a flapping bird, and emitted his loudest and meanest growl. Roo immediately joined in with bared teeth and her own interpretation of her meanest growl as she pulled Mitch towards her foe.

We can take him. I've had enough of this dominant stuff. I want him now! But Mitch wouldn't let Roo have at it. His flapping arms and inhuman voice scared the dog away, leaving the two of them in the middle of the road. *How did you do that?* Roo inquired with her eyes as she looked up at Mitch. *Maybe, one of these days, you won't scare him away so I can finally eat him?*

She felt a slight tug at her collar and heard Mitch call to her. She turned away from the fleeing dog and followed. The two continued their rhythmic duet towards the route's final turn. Again, complete silence except for the sounds of running shoes and paws hitting the pavement. It was bliss to the both of them.

Approaching the last leg of their route, Roo's cadence began to slow. Her paws began to drag as the tired look of age entered her eyes. Though a mind of Roo's vintage can run fast forever, a body of Roo's age, unfortunately, cannot. *I hate this,* she thought. *I used to be so good at this. I want to be* that *good again, but for some reason, I can't.* Her tongue hung a little further out of her mouth. *Even though it's hard, I still love to run. I do!*

Instead of cruising down the final incline before their right turn and the one mile climb towards their home, Roo suddenly found herself running behind Mitch. *I might be slow right now, but I know what's around the corner*, she said to herself. *Definitely! I hear it so clearly now… There's refreshment ahead. And after, I'll do my best to run fast again!* inferred the canine as her eyes widened and her tongue hung out of her mouth a little bit further.

Mitch slowed his pace to match Roo's. They made the loop's final turn. The runner stopped by the side of the road, knelt down, unclipped Roo's leash, and pointed to the fast moving creek which meandered a few feet down the short ravine from where the two now stood. Roo knew exactly where to go. If she loved anything more than running, it was lollygagging all hot and tired into this refreshing swimming hole, flopping down on her belly in the water, and drinking in the nectar of the spring's coolness. After those first few sips, to say she had a doggy smile on her face was a blatant understatement.

As he always did upon gazing at her smile, the runner smiled back, chuckled a laugh at the predictability of his best friend, and after a few minutes, called her out of the water. Knowing she had one more mile up a long hill to get back home, the refreshed yet tired dog reluctantly left her swimming hole. A creature of habit, Roo answered Mitch's glance and said to herself, *Before running, I have one more thing I have to do.* She left the water, moved up to her blissful plant covered flat spot next to the creek, flopped on her back, pointed her paws to the sky, and euphorically rubbed and rolled in the forest's underbrush.

Hearing her name call her back from her upside-down happiness trance, she trotted back up the ravine's wall, felt her leash click in place, and gave it her all to keep up with the runner next to her. *The swim definitely helped me, but I can't keep up with you anymore. Why?* She pondered. *Whatever. My job is to get you back home safely and that's what I'm going to do, regardless of how slow we do it.*

Her tail began to wilt like an under watered flower. She pushed on while the runner looked down at her. Locking his eyes, she felt an amazing sense of pride in being able to spend her entire life protecting her athletic friend while they ran together on the roads and trails around their home.

I can do this, Roo seemed to scream. *How many times have I run this hill? Just gotta keep moving... Moving... Panting... Running... Wait... STOP! This smells lovely.* She heard Mitch laugh to himself yet again. She looked up and saw him shaking his head. *I know what you're thinking, Daddy. We're traversing up a mile long mountain road and you're likely about to start babbling how momentum is the key for me to complete it.* She went back to sniffing as she continued her thoughts. *And then I stop to smell something only I find intoxicating. If you had my nose, you would stop, too.*

"C'mon Roo," she heard her friend say as she was gently pulled away from the goodness on the ground. *OK... OK, it's time to finish what we've started. Time for me to be the greatest running companion I can be.*

At first she trotted, but then found her inner strength and began to run up the steepest pitch of the hill. However, like a marathoner falling apart at mile twenty three, she felt her paws again begin to drag, yet she pushed on with true determination. *Oh, I don't want to be the slow one, but it's hot and I'm so furry, even though I've lost five pounds of hair throughout this heinous summer.* She did her best to telepathically communicate with Mitch as his concerned face looked down at her. *Just a little more... I can do this... I can do this...*

Digging even deeper to bring her daddy home safe and well exercised, she pushed herself from her tired trot and into the final gallop she instinctively knew would bring her over the crest of the hill and down towards the driveway. "C'mon, Roo!" she heard Mitch shout, knowing he must sound quite silly to anyone listening; his cheers similar to that of an excited varsity track coach at a state meet. The two pressed on as Roo's tongue extended even further out of her mouth to the point that Mitch thought she was going to trip over it. *I can make it… I can make it…* She ran harder. *Gotta keep up with Daddy…* "C'mon Roo!" Mitch shouted again.

Seconds later, like a heavenly plateau, more consistent than the ocean's horizon, more welcoming to a tired dog than maple smoked bacon, the road flattened, pointed a short distance downhill, and intersected with the driveway's junction where, just forty five minutes and four point two miles ago, the team embarked on their running adventure.

With her leash now unclipped, Roo stood panting and stared up at her daddy, not thinking, but only feeling. Feeling thanks. Feeling love. Feeling friendship.

After her customary post run binge at her water bowl, she slowly walked back to her nest under the crabapple tree, moved the topsoil around to get to the cooler earth underneath, laid herself down, reflected on what she had just experienced and thought, *I love having a Daddy who's a runner.*

~~~~~~~~~~~~~~

After unclipping the leash from her collar, Mitch watched as Roo trotted around to the backside of their house and towards her water bowl. He took off his belt, to which he had attached Roo's leash, and slowly meandered up the driveway, wiping sweat from his forehead as he moved. He stopped at the base of the stairs to the entrance of his home, put the toes of his left foot on the edge of the bottom stair, and stretched his calf in hopes of relieving the subtle pain in his shin. Twenty seconds later, he switched feet and stretched his right calf.

When the stretch was completed, Mitch looked up and involuntarily chuckled as he witnessed Roo come around the house, jowls dripping with the waters from her bowl. She walked past him, stopped under the crabapple tree, scratched and moved around the soft earth with her paws, and re-made her nest.

Nesting in the dirt, he said to himself. *One of these days, I'll join her when she does that!*

Pleased with her landscaped pillow creation, Roo made a few circles in the dirt, and plopped herself down. Mitch walked towards her. They made eye contact. Mitch smiled. Roo gave a big sigh and let her tongue slightly hang out of her mouth, knowing that in a few seconds she was going to get some love.

The runner sat down next to her and told her she was a good girl. Knowing she was further on in her years and didn't have too many runs left in her, Mitch said out loud, "Thanks for everything, Roo. Thanks for being such a wonderful companion and a great running friend." He scratched her behind her ears as he spoke. "Remember when you used to beat me up that hill hand over paw? You always made it look so easy." A few moments passed. "But now, it's like you've given me your strength."

Mitch continued to pet her as he reflected on what he just spoke aloud. He seldom timed himself running up the mile long hill, but knew in his heart and by the effort, which he had just put forth, that his training was making him much stronger. He thought about his speed workouts on the horse track, the trail runs in his mountainous backyard, and his tuned focus on hitting a PR in October. As his mind wandered, he envisioned himself racing towards the finish line and catching a glimpse of the clock as he approached it. *3:25 and some change*, the runner thought. *I'd be so elated if I could pull that off!*

A scratching feeling on his arm snapped him out of his trance. He looked down to see Roo pawing at him as he realized that somewhere during his thoughts, he had stopped petting her.

"I'm sorry, girl!" he responded as the petting commenced again. "I just spaced out. There I was thinking about how fortunate I've been to be able to run with you over the past ten years and my ADD kicks in." He bent over and kissed her between her ears. "Silly Mitch." Roo's tongue gently licked her jowls in a show of thanks that the petting continued. They sat in silence this way for a few minutes.

"It sucks you're getting slower, Roo," Mitch said. "Just when I'm hitting my groove and running the best I've ever run, you have to get old on me." He paused for a few moments. Images of a not too distant world without Roo tried to invade his space. He pushed back, not allowing the negative thoughts to overtake the happy moment of shared solitude.

"You're such a good girl, Roo," the runner said. Roo acknowledged him with another deep sigh and shut her eyes. Mitch kissed her head, gently gave her one last pet from her neck to her tail, and quietly rose from his friend's sleeping spot. As he tiptoed away from her and towards the steps of his home, he couldn't help but stop, turn around, sneak a glance at the wonderful sleeping animal under the tree, and thank the Universe for bringing her into his life.

8

Balance

The early morning runners chased each other through the thick sea fog, each appearing as if they were ghosts flying out of the unknown. The heavy air, thick with the ocean's scent of Portland's still, calming harbor, overwhelmed each runner's senses to the point where it felt like they were gliding along the water's surface instead of on the adjacent paved path. Sounds of fog-hidden, motivated workers pulling boats out of the water in advance of the slow-approaching hurricane accompanied the group of two hundred as they progressed along the course of the morning's 10K relay.

Leaving the commercial docks and yacht services area behind, the path continued straight, parallel to the antique train tracks and adjacent to the jagged, rocky shoreline. To the left was a sixty foot high cliff that was lined with thick vegetation, each leaf tickled by the drops of moisture floating in the air. To the right, just off the path, was a ten foot craggy drop off to the water. A couple sat on the furthest point off the small jetty, dangling their legs off the rocky edge while enjoying their morning coffee in the fog. Clearly not having known about the race before choosing their quiet morning's vista, they looked up with smiles and laughter that told us of their wonder and disbelief as the pack ran by.

A few hundred feet further down the path, just past the steel sculptures depicting scenes of life at sea, the harbor's jetty sloped to an inviting beach, a patch of sand only twenty feet wide from the path to the water, yet stretching out almost a quarter of a mile into the distance. Barefoot children ran around on the sand experiencing the bliss of testing the cold sixty-degree waters with their toes. Squealing with laughter, they each, in turn, ran back to their parents, their feet thick with wet sand as their toes quickly returned to normal body temperature. Dogs swam after tennis balls and sticks further off the short beach as kayakers maneuvered around each canine's focused trajectory.

Most racers wore ear buds, choosing to give the race its own personal soundtrack. A minority of the athletes instead chose to be inspired by the sounds around them. Running in the front third of the pack of racers, Mitch chose the latter, tuning himself to his body's rhythms while simultaneously meditating on the beauty that surrounded him. Moving along the mystical course, he unconsciously let himself feel small in the vast expanse of the universe as the fog enveloped the waterfront. As he raced along the narrow path, it became effortless to let himself cascade off the edge of reality and into a blissful and weightless world.

After several minutes of running in this dreamlike state, Mitch reached the parking lot and the entrance to the beach. Here, the course took the runners to the left, over the train tracks, and away from the jagged coastline and the harbor it nestled. It then meandered up the switch-backed hill and towards the elevated promenade. The road's steep pitch pulled Mitch out of his trance as his body required a conscious effort to race up the incline. Breathing heavily as he climbed, the runner thrust his arms forward and back to mimic the pistons of the antique narrow gauge railroad engines, which now rested peacefully next to the old pier. He took inspiration and drive from these sleeping machines, whose power used to pull tons of cargo along these same coastal shores so many years ago.

The low fog thinned as the racers gained altitude. Through the runners' gasps and laboring breaths, Mitch could just barely hear someone strumming a guitar at the top of the hill. As he got closer to the music's source, he spotted where the acoustic melodies and on course entertainment were coming from: Joe, a.k.a Old Port Joe, the vagabond singer who would wander around the Portland waterfront giving impromptu concerts to anyone willing to listen. While loading out from a show just a few weeks back, Mitch stopped to listen.

The recognition immediately made him smile. "Johhhhh," he voiced at the highest volume his hard working lungs would allow as he crested the top of the hill, pumped his fist in the air, and received an equally enthusiastic reaction from the street singer clothed in stereotypical ripped jeans, oversized sweatshirt, and crooked baseball cap. "You rock!" screamed Mitch as he ran by him.

The musical motivator now behind him, along with the very conveniently placed top of the hill water station - water that Mitch considered best used for pouring over his overheated head on a hot summer morning - he pushed his lanky body along the promenade. Now above the thicker fog at an elevation of a hundred feet above sea level, the runner looked left and, through the breaking fog, was able to make out Peaks Island, Great Diamond Island, Little Diamond Island, and Fort Gorgeous, each spit of sand, rock, and trees, viewed as a sepia toned silhouette over the silver ocean. Above the black and white landscape, the sun made itself known, yet only as a partially obstructed sphere. Choosing instead to enhance the fog rather than break through it, its powerful rays reflected off the water molecules in the air giving the world around Mitch the feel of a washed out watercolor painting.

Just beyond this first group of islands, Mitch could just barely make out the sounds of the diesel engines of the lobsterman pulling their traps out of the water. In tandem with the glug-glug-hum of the lobster boat engines were the abrasive calls of the flocks of hungry seagulls that inevitably followed the working boats around. *That's hard work to be pulling so much gear out of the ocean before a hurricane,* the runner thought to himself, followed by, *almost as hard as this pace I'm keeping up!* Mitch then stole a glance at his watch. If he could keep up his 6:30/mile pace, he would be at the finish line and relay handoff in just under ten minutes.

As he coasted along the elevated flat section of the course, he thought about how much he loved running these shorter races during the months of his marathon training. They seemed to push him to do the harder and faster three to six mile quick tempo runs he had consistently found himself blowing off. He knew these always-difficult workouts were necessary to build his strength, yet when his training plan called for him to execute one, Mitch would often find the excuse to not do them; his rationale being that if he wanted to exercise his aging dog around his busy gig schedule, he didn't have the time to do all the training runs his plan suggested. His choice, time and again, was to take Roo for a mellow run.

However, for some magical reason, when he pinned a number on his shirt, inspiration to run as fast as he could had always manifested itself in his competitive mind. After blowing off several of his scheduled fast and speedy tempo runs dictated by his training plan, he had decided that his compromising solution to get a few hard effort runs in during his training was to race a shorter distance once a month. Moreover, the shorter distance races let him take inventory of his body and where he physically stood. After racing the morning's relay, he would capture and measure his fitness in one convenient moment, just seven weeks prior to Chicago's start.

As the course banked right, away from the water, and headed past the city's World War II monument, he let his mind wander over the current state of his body's fitness level. Midway through his marathon training, he weighed in at one hundred and fifty seven pounds and stood at roughly five feet, ten inches. He felt strong, yet at the same time, weak... Toned, yet at the same time, flabby. In short, he was confident, yet confused on how he should feel about where his current fitness level measured. Over the past few months, he'd been doing some pull-ups on a climbing piece that was mounted over his bedroom door, but could never quite get into the repetitive groove of sticking to the exercise... To really tone his upper body with the hopes of building the strongest core possible.

Though he knew each set of pull-ups would only take a few minutes and ultimately make him stronger, he found it easier to let his laziness prevail. Two out of three days a week, he would look at the pull up bar and walk right past it, always rationalizing that he worked out his body in alternative ways. To Mitch, his fitness was maintained four to seven times a week by repetitively packing and unpacking his truck of what he considered "really good sounding, but unfortunately very heavy gear." When he would look at the pull up bar on days he knew he'd be lifting gear and performing later that day or into the night, he would often substitute his gig for the workout. *I have no idea if lifting gear is an equal substitution,* he said to himself as he raced along. *It's just so damn hard pushing myself to do workouts that I don't enjoy doing.*

Banking left once again and passing the backside of the large microbrewery tucked in between the surrounding three-story apartments, he headed downhill towards the city's waterfront district. As he ran, the intensity of the exhaust from the fryolators from the restaurants that lined the city's street grew with each downhill step. Knowing the insatiable fried seafood each kitchen was preparing, Mitch's mouth began to water as he passed the historic brick buildings with attached patios and decks.

Oh, to lose those elusive five pounds would really help my speed, was the next statement to pop into his head as he thought about how many times when, while setting up for a show and eating his complimentary lunch or dinner, he'd often give his half empty plate back to the server with its staple eaten, but fries remaining. "Fries make me fat," he would say to the server after they would ask why he hadn't eaten any.

The runner shook his head at how many times he had said this to his co-workers. He then surprised himself when he said aloud, "I'm such a hypocrite!" as he replayed the multiple times this conversation occurred; each time he would return his plate of fries, it was minus some very yummy and unhealthy deep fried buffalo chicken fingers.

Choice and rationalization, Mitch said to himself. *To want to be that well disciplined and invincible athlete, but to also taste the yumminess of fried food smothered in hot sauce. To want to build my body to its strongest potential, but to instead embrace my laziness.*

As he rolled this thought around in his head, he couldn't help but compare the effort he put into being the best runner he could be vs. the effort of being the best singer he could be. Running and singing to his best potential each required its own version of hard work and sacrifice.

To professionally sing to thousands of people at a weekend festival or to five people at a bar on a Tuesday night, his breath control had to be maintained, vocal warm ups were not an option prior to performing, diet needed to be adhered to so there would be no congestion inhibiting his voice, stamina needed to be maintained, microphone control was a subtle necessity, and, most importantly, regardless of how he felt, when he stepped out onto any stage, he needed to be dead on. Whether a performer is singing on stage at Madison Square

Garden (someday) or at the local corner bar, there were no excuses. If Mitch wanted people to listen, he had to be perfect.

To race at an amateur level, his drive and motivation had to be just as consistent, yet there was more leeway in not adhering to what was required of him. He knew that he couldn't just check in to a marathon, as running twenty six point two miles required that he train hard and efficiently. Still, the only true competition for him was himself. No one would be watching him, judging him, or walking out of the room on him if he didn't perform well. The only person who would be happy or angry with him for hitting a PR or not doing well was himself. Moreover, he had a choice as to how happy or angry he would be if he hit or missed his goal.

"That's why running is harder than singing," his friend and former bandmate Dave had told him when Mitch first started to run marathons. "Even at the amateur level, musicians are expected to be spot on, where as runners are allowed more freedom. Nobody's counting on a runner's performance." As Mitch hit the bottom of the hill and made the left turn on the short segment of India Street, he let his memory of his conversation with Dave continue to preach to him. "It's interesting to think how running is personal. Music is very public. Running is more intrinsically motivated and therefore harder to sustain than music."

You could say that again! Mitch thought to himself as the course made a right turn onto Commercial Street and into the race's flat and fast last mile. As the runner absentmindedly picked up his pace, his dichotomous mind, again, told him that he was kicking ass, yet he should be kicking ass even more if he were to work harder. He had an idea how super fast racers trained, but was forced to accept that singing as much as he did allowed him only so much time to invest in his fitness.

His solution to readying his body for a marathon while simultaneously singing his heart out during his training journey was a plan he had come across in a running magazine. It insisted that three quality runs a week is all one needs to race twenty six point two miles at one's best speed. The one part of this plan, however, which Mitch had decided not to pay attention to, was that it also called for cross training - biking, hiking, swimming, etc. - on off days; to the singer, there was no such thing as an off day. *If I were to cross train like my training schedule says, the success of my running and my gigs would be comparable to racing the Indy 500 with a go-cart*, he thought to himself as he passed yet another restaurant emitting delicious fryolater fumes. *I'd be exhausted.*

To the musician, being a feeble player was out of the question. He wanted to rock. When his training plan's first scheduled twenty miler fell during a week which he had seven shows booked, he was forced to do his long run the morning of a late night four hour solo show. This had made his time on stage difficult, tiring, and his performance sub-par. If he wanted to enjoy both singing and running, he'd have to run long on days that had no scheduled shows.

I can't run long and gig in the same day. It makes me feel half empty on stage... And it sucks to suck, the runner said to himself as he approached the two and a half mile mark. *Gigging has to be my cross training for my off days*, he continued. *And I think it's working. Thanks to singing so often, my diaphragm is the strongest muscle in my body... And my breath control during my long runs has become so efficient.* To put an exclamation point on this thought, the runner, again, picked up his pace another notch.

But like a doctor hitting the reflex bone on his knee, his mind couldn't help but to involuntarily play the self-doubt card. He began to debate with himself that his choice was simply taking the path of least resistance. In blowing off the suggested cross training and embracing what seemed easiest, he might not be able to tackle the difficult goal of racing to his fastest potential in his upcoming marathon.

I know it feels like I'm being lazy, but I don't want to show up at Chicago's starting line exhausted, injured, or both, he said to himself. *I need to train the way it fits in with my lifestyle, even if I stray from the plan from time to time. I'm still working hard and giving it my all.* He pondered this for a few moments and then repeated what his great friend Janet had suggested to him on a run they did a few years back: "Training plans are only a guide. Life happens. Don't stress it. Enjoy the journey."

I have smart friends was his next thought as he shortened the distance to the finish line by a quarter of a mile. Two racers then startled him out of his mental retreat as they galloped past him, snapping him back into the moment, to racing the race. Mitch surged, suddenly awoken from his contemplations and realized that in a minute, he'd be at the relay exchange.

He knew Dylan would be super excited to see him sooner than she expected to. He had told her, before the start of the relay, that due to his lack of sleep and energy drain from last night's gig, he didn't think he had better than a 7:00/mile pace in him. He smiled at how his body had surprised him as he made a beeline towards his finish. In addition to passing a few more runners, he galloped ahead of one of the two racers who had recently past him.

As he raced towards his wife and the crowd of runners gathered at the relay exchange, he reminisced about the morning's memory of Dylan's eyes two inches away from his when he opened his... Her deep blue orbs of wonderfulness emitting all the energy a soul mate can give, staring deep into the reaches of his heart, intoxicating him to elation in his first seconds of wakefulness.

He sprinted the last forty yards to the finish at his strongest pace. Just before crossing the finish line, he spotted her, arms waving and her cheers permeating over the crowds roar. As fast as a shooting star appears and disappears from the night sky, he crossed the finish line, passed the relay bracelet to her and, before he had even a second to catch his breath, she was gone, running at her fastest pace, away from him and in the other direction.

As Mitch walked off the previous twenty minutes of effort, he wished there was time for a kiss at such a quick relay exchange, but he smiled to himself knowing that he'd kiss her sooner than later. He then moved through the crowd of cheering spectators, other finishers, and additional athletes awaiting their relay exchange. His cool down had to be quick since a stage was waiting for him in under ten minutes.

As he left the finish area and made his way towards his truck and his change of comfy dry clothes, his mind replayed last month's conversation with the Race Director. *I don't know what I was thinking when I said yes to running a race and then singing to the finishers,* he thought to himself after remembering hanging up his phone. *Kind of like a bad practical joke to play on my body. Still, singing after a race is the perfect cross training scenario for me, given that singing is my other sport.* He again smiled at his rationalization.

He arrived at his truck, opened the tailgate, and climbed into the empty bed. *I'm so glad I got here early to set up my gear before the race. It would suck to have to lift gear right now!* he thought to himself as he did his best to stop sweating like a mountain cascade after a heavy rainstorm. He slid into his lightweight and luscious cotton gig clothes while doing vocal warm ups and mentally preparing himself for the stage.

Once changed, he climbed out of the back of the truck and took the longer route to the performance area, making sure to stop at the food station to inhale a banana, two slices of pizza, and a quart of water. Appetite quelled for the moment, he walked onto the stage and picked up his acoustic guitar. While tuning his Martin and quickly doing a line check to make sure his microphone and guitar were properly amplified, his race's internal debate seemed to reach its conclusion as an incredibly fortunate thought suddenly popped into his head.

It's all about balance. The thought made Mitch stop what he was doing. He took a deep breath and stared at the crowd of runners he had just raced against. *Yeah, balance,* he confirmed. *Just gotta keep the balance in my life happening... Just gotta keep doing what I'm doing.*

He first looked out over the waterfront and then closer towards the crowd that came forward to join him in music. His positive energy resonated off of the buildings and through the downtown area. As he began to sing, all Mitch could think about was how lucky he was to have combined so many loves into one awesome morning.

Beach

T he waves crashed onto the sandy shoreline. Each impact released a burst of aromatic sea salt over the vast expanse of the crowded, white-sand beach. Watching gravity's undertow pull the receding waters back into the next oncoming surge, the singer was reminded of his childhood when he would endlessly dive into the waves so he could ride them to back to shore. The warming sun, the taste of the saltwater, the feelings of not caring why his lips were blue or his fingers shriveled... Only caring about being perfectly placed in the water when the next big wave came so he could ride the jubilation to shore... And then do it over and over again.

Standing a few hundred feet back from the breaking waves, he grinned and shook his brain back to the present as he traded glances with the audience, the waves, and the needle on the guitar tuner he was currently working. It was a beautiful day, one in which the cobalt blues of the warm afternoon's summer sky were perfectly fractured by a few dancing puffs of interspersed white. Such a day would ensure that both he and all the folks around him would harbor their smiles long after the sun set.

After kneeling down to sip from the beer that a very friendly couple had bought for him, he continued to work his guitar's six strings back to a tuned 440 Hz. While doing this, the sounds of the waves, the crowd's chatter, and an airplane's propeller filled the audio void. The singer looked up at this last sound and saw a large, lazy single propeller plane dragging a hovering advertisement over the ocean's horizon. The banner implored the large crowd at Old Orchard Beach to heed its floating message and finish off the afternoon's festivities by savoring a "$10 lobster roll at Bay Haven Seafood, Route 1, Saco."

From Mitch's perspective, he seemed to have the perfect vantage point to view the scenery around him, even though he was only elevated ten inches off the ground. To his back, the hotel's five stories greeted the sky like a perfectly fitted puzzle piece. Over him hung a large awning that sheltered his fragile acoustic instrument, his thumping PA, and his exposed bald head from the sun's powerful rays. In front of him, on the large patio and just before the start of the sandy beach, sat a few hundred vacationing beach bums, each enjoying the vibe of the afternoon while seated at the patio bar or at one of the pub's outdoor high top tables.

It was a fun crowd to watch. To the singer, being on stage was the best people watching experience one could get. He couldn't help but notice the single guys trying their best to act nonchalant as the bikini clad girls they bought drinks for smiled back at them, consciously harnessing their sexuality. He watched parents who were gathered around the larger tables do their best to control their kids from leaving them so they could either play on the beach or get closer to the stage. He witnessed other groups of friends emit auras of joy towards each other as they sipped their beers or rum drinks, their elation magnified by listening to good live music while basking in the sun's warming light. Mitch always loved this gig.

Temperatures were in the nineties when he had loaded his three hundred and fifty pounds of gear onto the stage. It caused the top of his head to emit sweat in a similar pattern to exploding fireworks - ten to twelve different lines of moisture consistently cascaded down his head with each piece of gear moved. Still, he embraced the heat.

He had worked efficiently at setting up his PA and, given how his marathon training had developed his endurance, had just sang amazingly strong for an hour and forty five minutes. Though he prided himself on loving his time on stage, with each passing minute during his long set, all he could think about was how great it was going to feel when he strummed the set's last chord, placed the guitar back in its stand, turned the set break music on, dashed to the bathroom to change into his swimsuit, and finally made the mad sprint onto the beach with nothing to think about except the soon to be reality of being underwater.

"Ziggy Stardust," was Mitch's choice for his first set's last song. *Quick, easy on my voice, enjoyable for all. Yeah, "Ziggy,"* he thought to himself. "You guys have been a lot of fun to sing to!" Mitch said into the microphone. "I'm gonna do one more song and then jump in the ocean. Anyone feel like joining me?" The singer laughed knowing that not every musician gets to say something like this to a crowd. "My name is Mitch. I've got another long set coming up after my break, and I hope y'all stay for the duration. Thanks again for your smiles!" With his guitar now in tune and his throat watered to his satisfaction, he strummed a hard G chord to start the final song of the set.

Utilizing the patio's surface, he sang to the crowd with an added passion knowing that his listeners went further than the edge of the restaurant's boundary. He loved that his music reverberated off the patio's hard concrete floor and out over the landscape's white sands, throwing the melodies of voice and rhythm to the many sunbathing people stretched out beyond him.

How many times have I played this song? he thought to himself as he strummed the song's introduction. *Let's see, I'm forty one, I started playing this tune when I was twenty, I must have sung it ten to fifteen times a year until I went full time music four years ago, which now has me singing it about a hundred and fifty times a year, knowing that I try not to sing it at every gig, brings it to a total of...* he forced himself back to the moment. *Mitch! Can you please concentrate on what you're doing!* he yelled at himself. *You* are *performing in front of a few hundred people!*

As the first verse of the song came around, his mind continued to wander while his voice worked the microphone. Several months ago, he had realized that playing long sets elicited the same out of body experience that he had learned to embrace during his long training runs. During these long runs, when his body unconsciously fell into its good groove, it somehow became a machine that performed incredibly well on an involuntarily level, thus giving the feeling of his mind leaving his body. When this would happen, his body would somehow perform practiced, effortless, and true, even though he was in the middle of a hard workout. Because he put the same amount of passion into singing long sets as he did running long training runs, this similar experience now happened to him on stage.

He began to ponder how the body became so tuned into what is happening that he could suddenly forget what's happening... So he could think about everything else that's happening. "So where were the spiders..." Mitch sang, sarcastically thinking how he just came up with a thought that mentioned "happening" three times in a philosophically waxing way while rocking out such a timeless song.

Almost to the song's close, he made eye contact with a group of folks on the far side of the patio. He was psyched they were looking at him and singing along rather than facing the other way and looking at the beach. His voice felt great. His stamina was dead on. His singing and playing were both fluent and easy.

"Ziggy playyyyyyyyyyyed... Geee-tahhhhhhhhhhhhhh." Not even sixty seconds after strumming the closing chord and again thanking the crowd, Mitch was on the beach. The sand, just off the patio's concrete and a long fifty yards up from the ocean, burned his feet almost to the point of being uncomfortable. Knowing such a sweet experience doesn't happen in Maine most of the year, he took note not to take the pringling feelings of the warm sand around his feet for granted. In two steps, his walk became a slow sandy run.

He slalomed through the scattered piles of people, towels, umbrellas, and kids digging their holes. "Hey, it's the singer guy!" said a sun bathing girl as his quick left turn brought him around yet another hole, this huge one likely dug by a parent. "I can't wait for water!" Mitch said back to the girl as he cornered around one last group of sunbathers.

The ocean, now only twenty feet away, cooled and hardened the moist sand as the low tide slowly moved out, pushing and pulling the ocean in the endless cycles of the moon. With no more obstacles in front of him, he sprinted. Knowing how silly and goofy he looked when he finally hit the water's edge, yet not caring, he continued his drive to get deep enough to dive in. He thought to himself, *If my price for playing music at the beach is being laughed at by fellow beach goers, it's all good!*

He chased a receding wave that lured him to run even further out. The softness of the cold and muddy sand underneath the two feet of water he was running in quickly cooled him from his spine to his fingertips. After a few more dopey hurdles over smaller incoming waves, the invigorating salty smells overwhelmed him. He hurdled another small wave.

Now waist deep in the water, a big wave loomed ahead. He pointed his body into a dive position and launched himself forward as the wave broke over him. *KA-SHOOOOOOOOOO* was the sound the water made in his ears as his body disappeared beneath the ocean's surface… Bliss.

He had always loved that sound, that indescribable tone he heard when he dove into a breaking wave. The taste of the salt mixed with the liquid gold of the sea immediately gave him a combination of relief, release, and pure gladness.

His head broke the water's surface. He pointed his nose towards the sun. He next turned towards the shore, looked at the hotel he'd been singing at, and though he had done it hundreds of times before, he felt compelled to again say out loud, "Thank you" to no deity in particular. *Just a random thanks to whatever or whoever for allowing me to lead this life*, was the thought that followed.

Aside from being amazing relief for an overheated singer, Mitch also knew how beneficial the cold water could be to an athlete whose body isn't functioning at one hundred percent. As this thought entered his mind, he involuntarily reached down and began to massage his aching shin. He thought back to how this annoying, minor injury had crept up on him since he had ramped up his training. Running hard had taken its toll on his body similarly to the way the summer sun slowly bleaches the color out of stained wood.

Doing his best to work the ocean's cold magic into his bones, he thought about how, during last November's running of The New York Marathon, Dylan's time had qualified her for the following spring's running of the Boston Marathon. Mitch didn't qualify, but he wanted to assist his honey through the winter's training even though running hard through the winter was very new to him; his winter passion had always been to strap a couple of skis onto his feet and rip down a double diamond trail while drawing multiple perfect S shapes in the snow with a telemark skier's calligraphy.

But to qualify for Boston, to Mitch, was an amazing accomplishment. He couldn't be more proud of his wife. His drive to assist her with loving companionship during her long runs on fifteen degree mornings on snow covered roads couldn't be more resolute. Additionally, he didn't want to lose the fitness he had gained and utilized during his 3:27 New York race.

Soon after Dylan's qualifying run, he read a blurb in "Runner's World" about how a fellow marathoner maintained her fitness: Train all year. *This could prove to be fantastic for both Dylan and me,* he had thought as he perused the magazine after waking one very cold winter morning, the smells of the wood stove's endurance standing strong against the night's frigid winds. *Train all year. It seems so obvious,* he had thought.

By the time Mitch had decided that Chicago would be his next race, a distant six months from the gun going off, he was already doing fifteen milers at his ½ marathon race pace. He was repeatedly throwing his body up and down the steep hills of Maine's back roads, embracing the shadows of the leafless trees, chasing the sun over the crests of the road, and flying wonderously through the pavement's next twists and turns.

To a smart marathoner, running this hard so long before a race is not sustainable. But an athlete can only learn how far he can push his body by taking it to the limit, and sometimes going over it.

After Dylan's race came and went, Mitch continued to push himself. One early summer afternoon, the bugs and humidity had been equally oppressive in the foothills he called his home. Respite from both often came from the coastal roads just a short hour's drive from his front door. The sea breeze had been perfect, the biting deer flies were left in the foothills, the afternoon clouds had obscured the blazing sun above, the fragrance of the sea rose bushes and salty air had offered a cocktail of serenity.

He had been out for seventeen miles at what he truly thought to be an undemanding stride. His mind, as it often did during these long runs, had exited his body and was busy going over the musical pre-production he would need to accomplish when he returned home. However, like a splinter which slowly works its way underneath the skin, the first feelings of aggravation had manifested itself in his right shin, causing his mind to quickly snap back into the moment.

Much the same as so many runners he'd often spoken to in the past, he had shrugged off this new pain and recanted to himself the rumour that marathoners who trained hard were supposed to be in pain. As he ran on, however, he knew in his gut that this pain was different. This time, he didn't feel hurt. He felt injured.

The run completed, recovery drink consumed, and dry clothes in place on his body, Mitch drove home while wondering what his next step should be. His biggest question was how to continue to train hard while healing the pain in his shin. He knew, deep in his heart, that if he didn't approach healing the right way, the slight pain would grow, expand, and ruin his goal of making a great record and running a strong marathon all in the same week.

He had figured speed workouts on the soft dirt of the fairground's horse track would help lessen the impact of his footfalls. Runs with Roo would hold him back and prohibit him from racing from telephone pole to telephone pole. And of course, every distance runner's good friend: the ice pack. Several months had cycled by, the injury still there but, to a runner living in a world of rationalization, somehow had been kept in check.

Now, sitting in the ocean's frosty medicinal waters and massaging his shin, he embraced all the goodness the day offered. He managed to shrug off all fears that a bothersome injury might keep him from achieving his upcoming goals. *It is what it is*, he told himself. *It doesn't feel any worse than it did when I first felt it, so I've got that going for me… Which is nice.* He took a deep breath, stopped his massage, and stood chest deep on the ocean's floor. *I'm just going to keep doing what I'm doing and do my best*, was his next thought. Though a simple statement, it felt incredibly important to him.

The singer checked his watch. It was getting time for him to head back to the stage and rock out to the many folks awaiting his return. He turned towards the shore. He let a swell rise from behind him. He stood steadfast in the suction of the tide as the wave's undertow did its work to pull him out to sea. Leaning forward just a bit, he kicked, found the sweet spot of the breaking wave, threw his arms forward, lowered his head, and moved with the moon's force as his golden body surged through the clear waters with the fast moving wave towards the shore's edge.

Lying on his belly on the shoreline and giggling with the thrill of the ride he had just taken, he admitted to himself how much fun it was for him knowing that the skill of a ten year old could still make a forty one year old feel so good. Refreshed, humbled, and content, the singer exited the water and jogged back up the beach. As he left the sandy beach and stepped onto the patio, his next thought was, *it's gonna be a really great second set!*

10

Long

T he hummingbird glided effortlessly towards the window feeder. The ruby colored feathers on his neck reflected true elegance in the glass as he hovered over the artificial flower and drank in the sweet nectar provided for him. Standing on the opposite side of the window, which the feeder was mounted on, Mitch involuntarily smiled the way he always did when he witnessed these beautiful creatures visiting his home.

As the aroma of his morning's first cup of coffee complimented the magic of the hummingbird's visit, thoughts of the day's long run entered his mind. These were good thoughts. It was Tuesday. He woke this morning feeling both rested and centered, as it was a rare occasion for him to have two consecutive days off during the summer's busy gig season.

Twenty, today, he thought to himself. He had to laugh at the thought of running solo for such a distance. Though he had completed long runs of this magnitude many times before, the motivation to get himself out the door for such an endeavor consistently overwhelmed him. "Yeah… Twenty today," he said out loud to the drinking bird, giving the distance even more gravity.

The runner began to mentally go through his checklist of preparedness. *All carbed up with last night's pasta, gotta fill the*

Camelback with electrolytes, must, must, must not forget the Body Glide, three to four energy gels for the run, an extra layer in the pack in case it rains... he thought to himself.

"And then go," he said out loud as if speaking the thought would help him commence his day's undertaking. Though he felt thankful to have a couple of days off, the fact that he had no scheduled gig to be at after his run caused him to procrastinate in getting his workout started.

His thinking trailed off from his day's priority as he watched a second hummingbird dive bomb and buzz his counterpart away from the window feeder. Seconds later, the buzzing bird was buzzed himself. As he watched the birds taking their turns at the feeder, he felt incredibly fortunate to be able to live in a place where hummingbirds lived their lives just outside of his back door.

A few sips of coffee later, he turned, walked into his kitchen, and prepared himself the most balanced and sustaining breakfast he could possibly ingest: a scrambled egg on a toasted bagel. He knew it would ride the edge of feeding him until full, but one which he could digest quickly and wouldn't hurt his belly during his three or so hours of exercise. Once accomplished, he poured himself a second cup of coffee, left the kitchen behind, and walked towards the back door and the bustling bird feeder.

Stopping a few inches from the window, his mind began to churn. *Where do I want to run today?* he asked himself. As he thought about the many routes he had to choose from, each a unique combination of roads, trails, hills, and flats, he let his running focus slowly erode as his fascination with hummingbirds became an easy diversion.

He savored his second cup of coffee but couldn't quite enjoy it to its fullest while his buried enthusiasm was mentally beating him up for his procrastination skills. While absorbing the blows, he reflected on how much he loved his solo time even though he sometimes regretted that it fell during the workweek, when no one was available to go long with him. *I could sure use a friend to help me get this run underway,* he thought to himself. His life, so hinged on time management and efficiency, would always fall away towards idling comfortably when no one else but himself was dependent on him.

All right, he said to himself. *Enough! Watching hummingbirds is fun, but I need to motivate before breakfast digests and hunger kicks in... But where to run?* As beautiful of a location in which he lived in, the one downfall it had to an athlete going long was the amount of relentless hills that surrounded his home. Steep, vertical inclines, which were surrounded by trees, always toyed with his mind; they never appeared as steep as the exposed rocky hills of the higher terrain, yet each time he would run up them, they were always exponentially more difficult than viewing them from below.

When his runs were under ninety minutes, he always enjoyed the alternating momentum of the local hilly terrain. But living at the top of a one mile hill with over eight hundred feet of vertical gain made it hard for him to stomach running long from his front door. *Running up Norton Road at mile twenty... I don't know.*

Since today's long run was the final twenty miler of his chosen training plan, he wanted it to be special. He thoroughly appreciated his previous mapped out routes, runs which included loops of rolling terrain off the main roads closer to town, the there and back long runs on the deliciously flat coastal roads, and the lollipop routes that combined dirt roads and pavement.

He next thought of his amazingly strong wife and how she had trained for Boston the previous winter, each long run started and finished from their home. Over and over, she would wake, eat, and dive into the hills just off their driveway without giving a thought to the steep climb at her long run's finish. No matter how many times she did it, it always left Mitch awe-inspired that her twentieth mile was up the steep road that led to their front door.

Mitch! he yelled at himself, *You can do this! You've seen Dylan finish her long runs so many times with a huge smile on her face. Not even five months ago, you met her at mile ten for her last long run and witnessed how strong she finished. And you finished just as strong with her.* He continued to beat himself up. *The mile twenty hill is not a big deal. You know it's all mental.*

"It's all mental." How many times had he heard this before? Marathoners from around the world would often say this simple statement to each other whether their plan was to race a sub three hour marathon or to run the distance over a five and a half hour time frame. In the end, regardless of the projected finish time, the marathon inevitably hurt, always challenged, and was always hard. Thankfully, the human mind is extremely powerful and knows all too well how the body can sustain punishment through endurance. A focused athlete can become unstoppable and unbreakable - if she or he first believes it themselves.

Just a few nights ago, Mitch and Dylan had watched a documentary called "Running the Sahara." In the film, three nutty guys ran a four thousand five hundred mile route from Western Africa all the way to the Red Sea; it took them just over one hundred days to accomplish, each runner logging almost fifty miles a day over incredibly difficult terrain. Early in the film, as the director was interviewing the most hardheaded runner of the group, this very simple statement, "It's all mental," became the focus of the conversation.

"Anyone can run long... Anyone," the main character had said. "Running long is ninety percent mental." He paused, and then continued. "The other ten percent, well... That's all in your head!"

Mitch grinned to himself as he replayed this scene. He knew his fitness was where it needed to be to complete the day's long workout, even if it did roll up and down for twenty miles and would end with a huge hill. He also knew the primary obstacle for tackling this difficult route was, of course, all in his head.

Done! the now motivated runner thought as he turned his focused mind on his immediate task at hand. Within minutes, he was out the door, down his driveway, and running.

The late morning's breeze caressed his face with a softness akin to a butterfly's wings as it flies from flower to flower. The pavement responded to his running shoes with the similar effortless sensation of a trampoline bounce as the crisp, late September air filled his lungs with vibrant energy. It was great to be alive!

As he ran, the athlete heard nothing but the sounds of his footfalls. He gazed across the roadside pasture at the round peak of Sawyer Mountain, its lower elevations just starting to turn with the trees at the higher elevations, already a glorious façade of reds, yellows, and evergreens. Noting the season's change of color, Mitch began to descend the long hill he'd be running back up in what he hoped to be in just a little over three hours. He made an effort to shorten his strides as gravity went to work on his body, knowing that as easy as it was to fly down the hill, he'd need the energy reserves much later to climb back up.

Mile one completed and the long downhill stride now behind him, Mitch took inventory of his body. Even though he was getting stronger, three and a half months of solid training coupled with his idealistic train all year philosophy had taken its toll on his body. *Knees OK... I-T band good... Hamstrings holding up... Shin pain there, but certainly bearable,* he thought to himself as he made the run's first left turn onto Route 117.

His memory then danced back to last week. He had had a conversation with his friend Ellie while on a rest interval during a track workout. They had talked through their gasps of air after just completing a sixteen hundred meter sprint.

"My shin seems pretty good." Ten seconds of breathing passed. "But the pain is still there. I don't want it to be there," exhaled Mitch.

"Mitch, you did something to it," cough… "and you've been training hard on it for a half of a year." Ellie said as she tried to regulate her breathing. "But you caught the injury before it got bad. You've been smart and because of that, you can still race." After a long deep breath to bring her breathing back to normal she continued, "You're kicking ass on these sprints! Just don't do anything dumb, and you'll do great."

"Yeah… I know," replied Mitch. "But you know what happens late in a marathon." A few more seconds passed. "I hate what-ifs." Mitch looked at his stopwatch. "Let's start jogging. Twenty five seconds until the next interval."

"When I won my age group in last year's ½ marathon," Ellie reminisced, "I had so many things hurting me when I got to the starting line. When that horn went off, it was magical. All the pain seemed to vanish." They jogged in silence. A few seconds later she added, "Well, it came back at mile two, but it was neat for a bit."

"Ohhhhh, Ellie… To live in an idealistic world," Mitch replied with a sarcastic tone. "Four, three, two, one… GO!" And they sprinted.

Reliving this conversation as if it were more real than the run he was actually doing, he picked up his pace a few seconds/mile. He couldn't help but smile. The injury, which he previously thought was going to cause him to drop out of his race, had somehow regressed into a daily reminder that he was a hard working athlete. *How did I manage this?* he asked himself. *Concentrating on my form? Only running three days a week? Doing my short tempo runs on the trails?* He had no idea why his shin pain had dissipated to an annoyance during his last few weeks of training, but he wasn't going to question it. *Just hold it together. Who cares about the why? Roll with the moment and get into it. Ignorance is bliss*, he thought as his mind entered into The Zone.

For Mitch, twenty to thirty minutes into a long solo run, his mind would inevitably float into a different type of space. Time ceased to exist. His body became a well-oiled machine. His mind seemed to leave his body but remained tethered to it like a child carrying a freshly filled helium birthday balloon. His spirit seemed to look down at his physical form working beneath him as it monitored his body's athletic progress. Thoughts would flow in and out of his brain with molecular randomness. The Zone. Oh, how he loved it!

Forty minutes later, to his chagrin, as Mitch neared the busier intersection of Route 25, his spirit instantaneously retracted back into the physical as the need to be alert amongst the many oncoming cars and trucks became paramount. When his front door shut this morning, in order to ensure that he would avoid aggravating his shin or any other muscle during this last long run, he promised himself that he wasn't going to run faster than what he considered a mellow and leisurely pace. However, heavy traffic tossed this wish out the window, as his desire to make it to the route's next side street and off the busy road became his primary objective, one that required a speedy effort.

He used to be able to deal with running on main roads, but his tolerance for this was shot down several years ago when training for his first marathon. During the first eighteen miler of his running career, he had been at the turn around point of his chosen flat out and back route, nine miles from his vehicle. As the late spring skies opened up on him, he realized how completely unprepared to run in a cold and heavy rainstorm he had been. Moreover, as an inexperienced marathoner, he had neglected to pay attention to his pre-run nutrition and had quickly discovered how a significant lack of calories will cause the body to forget how to maintain a comfortable core temperature. Ninety minutes into the workout with another ninety to go, Mitch had found himself very cold, lonely, hurting, soaking wet, incredibly hungry, and losing all of his abilities to move forward. To add insult to his depleted hypothermic state, there had been nothing he could do except to keep moving towards his vehicle, whether by running, walking, or alternating between the two.

Though a rural thoroughfare with the same amount of trucks on the road every single day, during that very cold, raw, and miserable spring day, Mitch could have sworn there had been a semi-truck convention happening on Route 113 between Brownfield and Cornish. Endlessly, he had been getting splashed by the oncoming semis and their 55-mph sprays. What affected him even worse, however, were the repeated deafening sounds the trucks' huge dually tires had made as they rolled along the rain soaked highway. Each rotation had emitted deafening cries of high pitched squeals, which, to a runner whose body was breaking down, gave the feeling like glass was being crushed in his ears. It sucked.

He had wanted so badly for the experience to end. He had continually wished it would stop… Prayed for it stop… Yet had been unable to do anything about it. When he finally finished that painful and disastrous long run, he had promised himself that in the future, he would respect the long run, be smarter about his preparations for it, and wouldn't get stuck in such a position again.

With this memory still extremely fresh in his mind as he turned onto the bustle of Route 25, his mellow pace kicked into an all out sprint for the twenty or so minutes he was forced to stay on this overused highway. As he finally made the blissful right turn off the insanity and onto Route 5 and its rural wonderfulness, the runner slowed back his pace, again took inventory of his body, nodded to himself that all was good, and awaited his reclaiming of The Zone.

It was amazing to him how fast a super loud highway could be quickly silenced by the rolling terrain of a forested landscape. Within minutes, his footfalls became his audio focus as his route took him across the bridge of the Saco River and onto the dirt road that paralleled it's beauty. Seventy five minutes into his run, the lollipop part started, reminding him that when he passed this point on his way back home, his physical being would be a little different; his mind would need to work past his body's increasing pain, which would inevitably bear down on him like an anvil falling out of the sky.

The road meandered in tandem with the slow moving river. The Zone, again, overtook the runner. He reminisced about his prior three and a half months of training and how he had gotten to this point. He loved going long, but, to him, there was a certain kind of giddiness about the last long training run. He knew that when today's adventure was completed, there was going to be a much needed restful three weeks in front of him. *I love the taper of marathon training,* he excitedly said to himself, followed by, *Soon... So soon.* The anticipation of his well deserved, winding down of his hard training enhanced his desire to finish this last training run sooner than later.

As he ran, he couldn't help but to revel in the pleasurable consistency of the marathon training's journey... All the time, effort, and determination for just one race. *Amazing,* he thought to himself. *This is the fourth time I've worked my body at such an incredibly intense level... Just to race a hopeful three and a half hour race.*

The runner silenced his mind. He let his body work. From the spiritual perch above his physical self, he watched his tuned and fit body do its thing. *It's so addicting to feel myself getting stronger and faster,* he said to himself. *I love it.* Over the past few months, the runner had noticed how his body had strengthened, further took on a runner's shape, and, combined with his mind's need to approach everything he did with passion, had become a respectable running machine.

It's a constant journey which ultimately feeds my heart's growth, he told himself. He took ownership of this growth and pushed ahead knowing full well that the next time he was going to be out for this long, it would be at the thirty third running of the Chicago Marathon, a culmination of his efforts in addition to a celebration of the athlete he recognized himself to be on this beautiful early fall day.

As River Road forked and turned left towards the route's first large hill, Mitch said out loud, "C'mon body… We can do this!" The runner pulled an energy gel packet from his Camelback's pocket. He tore the top off the packaging, ingested the thick gooey substance, and winced at the burnt pudding aftertaste that inevitably came from each flavor; no matter how hard the manufacturers of these endurance products tried to make them taste good, to Mitch, they always had that awful aftertaste. To remedy the new dank flavor in his mouth, he drank a sip of his electrolyte-infused water from the tube that hung from of his slim backpack.

He looked up towards the top of Rocky Dunn Road. It wasn't a very long hill, only a third of a mile, but it was steep. There are often days when a long slow climb is preferred over the shorter, more vertical steeps, but since this was Mitch's last long training run prior to his race, one which he felt he had mentally conquered just by closing his front door behind him, a surge of power intoxicated him as he glided up the six hundred feet of elevation and took in the tremendous views of the northern Presidential Range of the White Mountain National Forest. *It's so cool that this is where I get to train!*

The runner frolicked the next half mile over the road's ridge and further down the longer mellow grade of the other side. He turned back onto Route 5 and glanced at his watch. *Wow, I've been out for an hour and forty five minutes and I'm feeling great,* he bragged to himself. *But I know what lays ahead,* the what being the oncoming tiredness, the self doubt as his body slowed, and the inevitable pain in his primary muscles. As he pondered the reality of what was to come, he made the conscious choice to force all negative thoughts out of his mind. To Mitch, in order to feel confident for his race, he would need to beat these obstacles in advance.

For anyone who wishes to not merely run a marathon, but instead strives to race the distance, the multiple long runs adhered to during the training program become exponentially necessary. To Mitch, as well as to marathoners around the world, in order to accomplish the marked difference between running a marathon or racing it, is to train hard on tired legs; to learn to engage one's secondary muscles after the primary muscles have broken down. And the only way to get one's legs tired so they can be trained to push through the pain is to run long distances over and over during the months prior to the race. During these long runs, when the inevitable feelings of lethargy and temptations to quit overtake the body, the real training begins.

This should happen just about the time I finish the lollipop part of the run and cross back over the Saco's bridge, the runner thought. *It'll likely be at about the two-hour-and-fifteen-minute tick of my old-school running watch.*

As the miles added on and conversations with himself careened through his head, the runner continued to embrace The Zone. However, his thoughts were somehow morphing into one of concern. His spirit, floating above his physical, witnessed his smiling lips shrink down and push together tighter. His brow began to furrow with concentration and focus. To keep on pace, he unconsciously dropped his shoulders and began to thrust his arms to assist in the rhythm of his running. "Bring it on," he heard himself mutter as he passed River Road, crossed back over the Saco River bridge, and ran towards the busyness of Route 25 and all of its loud cars and trucks.

Hearing the first distant rumble of a truck's engine, the runner smiled sarcastically to himself and shook his head. Even though he was going to be tired by the time he hit the intersection, he'd have no choice but to run hard on tired legs. His mind wouldn't let him relax with such an overload of vehicles around. *I knew this was going to happen... When did I become such a masochist?*

After turning left onto Route 25, Mitch had no idea how he had managed to make it through the next twenty five minutes. He was numb. Somehow, he had successfully blocked out the road's noise and was able to instead focus his mind inward. As he made the right turn onto Route 117 and towards his home, now just a short two and a half miles away, the runner felt himself reclaim his mind. He slowed his pace.

Though a short distance from home, he was more spent from the blind sprint on the busy highway than he cared to admit to himself. His lungs were burning. His quads felt like they were slowly filling with lead. A hunger for real food reminded him that he was now running on fumes, but the thought of eating another energy gel made his belly feel queasy. *Nothing to do but put one foot in front of the other,* he thought to himself and slowly ran on.

Around mile eighteen, Mitch began to experience a form of tunnel vision. It seemed to be caused by the narrowing of his tiring perception combined with the long limbs of the roadside oak and maple trees, which formed a nurturing domed canopy over the road. Though exhausted, he still managed to enjoy the serenity of the golden early afternoon sunlight reflecting off the autumn leaves. To the runner, it was as if the Goddess of the Trees knew what he was doing, and in a show of assurance, cradled him in her cool and shady arms.

Though he had just experienced a moment of bliss, he couldn't hold it as his body continued to tire. His mind, again, felt compelled to throw the weight of self doubt onto his positive thinking. As thoughts ricocheted uncontrollably in his mind, he admitted to himself that he was powerless to do anything about it. His brain was a gridlocked city intersection, traffic lights out, and un-policed.

Stay strong. I know... It hurts. But I have less than two miles and then I'm done! said the motivator inside him. Within a millisecond, the realist in him answered back. *If this hurts so much, why are you doing this? You're not going to win anything. It's still a great accomplishment to simply finish what's going to be your fourth marathon. Why do you have to train so hard to run fast?* The runner quickly answered his path-of-least-resistance thinking. *Because I want to be better than the last time! I don't want to go backwards. I want to grow. I want to PR. This is the only way. I have to earn it.* Rationalization rebutted. *But if you over work it, you'll injure yourself, maybe permanently... And then you won't be able to run any more. Why risk a lifetime of running for one fast race and a possible chronic injury?* The internal argument persisted over the rolling flats of his second-to-last mile. It was surely going to push Mitch over his mental cliff and towards his doom when, what he called an Exacto, occurred.

Exactos always made Mitch ponder the physics of reality. *Why, on a road with almost no cars, does an oncoming car always seem to cross paths with a car travelling from the other direction at the exact moment there's a runner alongside both of them... And always on a road with no shoulder,* he thought as he eyed the oncoming car, turned around, and eyed the car coming from behind him. As the Exacto happened, fear for his life caused the runner to leap off the road and into its drainage ditch in order to avoid getting hit.

Broken from his internal struggle and standing in the ditch, Mitch curiously looked up the three feet of dirt and further down the now empty road. As he scrambled back up the ditch and onto the road's six-inch shoulder, he realized how the last three hours of his mental ramblings were, in some strange way, amazingly good for his growth. *If running weren't a part of my life, I would surely drive myself crazy,* he told himself.

With a shake of his head and a spring of his step, he ran with an unexpected burst of adrenaline and determination. In just one and a half miles, his taper time would begin. Internal arguments now behind him, he cruised with a cool and easy stride towards the completion of his nineteenth mile. He turned right onto Norton Road and commenced with the long one mile climb to his front door.

He had run this hill hundreds of times. As the finish to the four point two mile loop he would regularly run with Roo, he would often sprint up its incline. He knew every angle of the climb, the crown of the road, and the shade of the trees at different times of the day. In fact, he knew this hill so well that he mentally broke it into parts and went so far as to name each section.

But today, the hill was new. It was the first time he would run it on very tired legs. Moreover, he let his adrenaline fuel the knowledge that when the last step of this run was completed, it would be the end of an eighteen week accomplishment. It would also be his first step towards healing his body in preparation for the twenty six point two mile journey that awaited him in three weeks.

The athlete attacked the incline with vigor similar to a champion Roman gladiator stepping onto the Coliseum's stage. His body, however, felt a little different than his ambitious mind. On the first incline, he immediately started to slow. He pushed harder, not paying any care to his lack of vertical speed. He found himself zigzagging up the steepest of the inclines the same way a backcountry skier would climb a mountain wall to lessen the risk of falling backwards and into the ravine. At other points, he walked while grunting and cursing the hill's unforgiving gradient. Still, he pushed on. He gained his inspiration from both the beauty of the mountainous surroundings and the knowledge that his front door was just over the next rise.

As the final crest of the hill came into view, "run fast on tired legs" repeated as a mantra inside Mitch's motivated mind. He took a deep breath, pointed his eyes forward, and with strength he didn't know he had, cruised the last one hundred yards to his home.

Finished. Mitch stopped.

He entered his driveway and walked up the dirt path and towards his front door. While doing so, he patted himself on his left shoulder with his right hand. "Good Job!" he said out loud. He took a long deep breath, thanked his body for being resilient, his mind for remaining focused, and the Universe for giving him such a beautiful place to train in.

Roo spotted him walking up the driveway and ran to greet her friend with the guilty eyes of a running partner left out of a long adventure. "You wouldn't have lasted past mile eight, Roo!" Mitch said to the inquisitive dog. "How about I give you a cookie and you won't be angry with me?" The dog's recognition of the word cookie and the knowledge that one was in her near future vaporized all elements of guilt as she led the way to the door.

Mitch turned the doorknob just three hours and nine minutes since he did the same to leave his home. As he entered his home and kicked off his shoes, he couldn't help but feel psyched with himself for such a strong effort.

The habit of his post long run routine played itself out with an automatic and seemingly easy effort similar to the way a scuba diver drift dives in an ocean current along a submerged reef. Within twenty minutes, he drank a quart of chocolate milk, ate a handful of peanuts and a banana, took a super sweet hot shower, and then proceeded to binge on a triple decker roast beef sandwich followed by a cold pint of good beer.

Fully engorged and close to catatonic, his thoughts drifted back to his upcoming race and how mentally prepared he had just become. If most of racing a marathon is run and fought in one's mind, he now had a memory to turn to if his body should want to quit.

As he lay down on his couch and stretched himself out, he acknowledged two things about how his mind and body felt after a long run. First, if a marshmallow had feelings, this is what one would surely feel like. Second, his will and determination were as hard as steel. Closing his eyes for his oncoming nap, his mind started to sing one of the songs he would be recording the day after tomorrow. Not even thirty seconds into the song, he was fast asleep.

Basics

"OK...rolling," the three players heard through their headphones as Jim, the engineer on the other side of the glass, released the talk-back button. He monitored the track's start time while focusing his eyes on the blank computer screen that would soon display Neil, Drew, and Mitch's audio colorations in the form of a musical graph.

The players focused their groove on the incessant tap, tap, tap, tap, tap of the metronome, which clicked in their headphones at ninety-four beats per minute. The band had always been challenged by this time keeper, otherwise known as the click track. For recording artists, it serves as the high wire they must walk in order to keep the tune aggressive, yet not too rushed... Just behind the beat, but not dragging. In order to create the foundation for a great song, it's up to each performer to internalize the right tempo and keep it consistent.

They've been recording, listening, strategizing, and recording some more for the past six hours. It was times like these that Mitch felt the mental exhaustion that he often experienced late in a long run. But because what had to be broken through was a barrier more of ego and art rather than the physical, it somehow seemed a grander challenge.

It's all mental, thought Mitch as he prepped to count off the song's next take, followed by the out of context thought, *It's amazing how the long run is similar to recording music.* As this side note entered his mind, the runner involuntarily embraced his marathon training and told himself, *Deep breaths, positive manifestations, smile! We have the power to make wonderful music*, was his next mental offering of confidence.

The click track persisted in their headphones, or cans, as Jim liked to call them. The rhythm section awaited Mitch's guitar intro. With Neil behind his drums and Drew wearing his bass, they both leaned in towards the guitarist, poised to give their all, similar to the way runners await the sound of the starting horn at the beginning of a race.

Drew, Neil, and Mitch approached the recording process with a mindset that bordered on telepathic. They each needed to be able to hear the same finished production of the song in their heads, though what their ears were hearing were instruments in their starkest forms... No sound effects, no bass and treble added, and with no lead vocal to make the song sound complete. In between takes, they talked about what the song's end result should sound like, but when the musicians were in the middle of playing a song while the bright red 'record' button was pressed, instrumental telepathy was all they had in order to communicate with each other.

To add to their challenges, each player needed to concentrate on how their parts synched up. As they focused on their own parts and simultaneously listened to each other's, communication was sometimes lost between them. This resulted in one or more of them screwing up, having to stop the take - regardless of how far they were into the song - and for the three of them to start over.

Because, some songs came together much quicker than others, it wasn't a surprise to them that after they had recorded their first song, "Middle of Nowhere" in forty five minutes, they had spent three hours on "Take it as it Comes" and were now two hours into "Move it Out," their third song of the day.

After many frustrating screw ups over a long recording session, just getting to the end of this final song would give them each a sense of euphoria. Fifteen minutes ago, when the last note of the previous take was played, each player had shared complete admiration for each other's talents because they had felt that they had just nailed it. After silence filled the room for several seconds and Jim signaled the recording had stopped, they had ripped their cans off their heads and dashed into the control room where Jim would play back the take.

For what seemed the hundredth time that day, pride had biased their ears and boosted their perceptions. They had entered the control room thinking that they had just completed a work of genius. But halfway through the listen, they reluctantly had to admit to themselves that the playback wasn't lying. Their take had not been the genius they had thought just a few moments ago. Reality told them the truth. Their ears could not escape it. What they had just recorded, in fact, sucked.

Upon closer inspection during another listen, this time with an inferred audience's perspective, they had heard how the second half of the song was rushed. The take was being played back through the studio monitors. Drew and Neil stood around the engineer's console while Mitch sang the song's lyrics from behind them. As Mitch sang the second verse, they had realized that what had sounded great just a few minutes ago - when the band was rocking without vocals - now sounded way too poppy for their tastes. Telepathy still at work, they had turned towards each other at the same time and said, "We need to do it again."

Through the revolving studio door, the players had made yet another solemn walk back out into the live room. They again talked to each other about the subtleties of how to make the next take a work of perfection, one that would execute the song's full vision.

Recording these guitar, bass, and drum foundation tracks, or basics as the recording world refers to them, simply put, are extremely difficult. Though the three of them had played these same songs over and over that day, the final result needed to give the listener the impression of a band walking into a room, picking up their instruments for the first time that day, rocking out a fresh, solid and amazing performance, putting their instruments down, and walking out. The completed recording must support the imagined perspective of how a rock band creates a great record - fluent and without effort.

With this thought on his mind, Mitch felt his soul settle into the tempo of the click track, just enough behind the beat to tame the aggressive rhythm of the song's introduction. "One, two, three, four," he counted off and kicked up the opening riff. Drew and Neil settled into Mitch's feel of the song, and after the four measure guitar intro, added their own hearts. Again, to the three of them, the vibe felt great. Their task was now to stay with it… To not obsess about their parts… To let things settle… To not push the tempo… To not screw up… To simply play the song the same way they've played it a thousand times… And to deliver a great performance. They've accomplished this twice already today, but fatigue was setting in and made them work harder at recording the keeper for this third track.

To Mitch, there was a certain beauty about the term "keeper" track. Being an independent artist, one who isn't signed to a lucrative recording contract, but instead pays for his records out of his own pocket, his recordings were done on a low budget. The gear went into the studio at the start of the day and was loaded out at the end of the day. When the day's session was completed, cash earned with the sweat of many shows would leave Mitch's hands. In return, an audio sample of a moment in time would be delivered back to him.

Because finances often hindered his ability to spend as many days as he felt necessary in getting the perfect performances down, what he and his band-mates would record today, this moment in time, was what both they and their fans would be listening to whenever they wanted to hear these songs. Solid musicians cannot overthink this. They must simply do their best to make a great recording. A keeper.

Three minutes and twenty seven seconds later, the players bit their tongues as the song's final note decayed to silence. Instruments and cans came off, and with another march through the door and into the control room, the three simultaneously held their breath, only to finally exhale when the playback button was depressed at the song's completion.

"Got it!" "Yes!" "Awesome!" Drew, Neil, and Mitch exploded and high fived each other while Jim hit the button to back up and save the day's third keeper track.

"Well, that took forever!" said Neil.

"But well worth the wait," answered Mitch as he smiled in the drummer's direction.

A certain kind of elation is often emitted from an artist when they realize they're contributing towards the making of a great record. This feeling generally mimics a well trained distance runner's perspective at the halfway point of a strong endurance race. He feels great, his body is working the way he's trained it to, he knows that there's hard work ahead, but he also knows that he's put in the time and training to confront the challenge... And is so excited for it.

At the end of the session, each player felt this way. As they broke down their gear and talked about the next steps of the recording, it reminded Mitch of the way he had calculated his pace in the middle of running the New York City Marathon and had realized that if he kept doing what he was doing, he would nail it.

After loading their gear out of the studio, the musicians stood by their vehicles and talked logistics about the CD's next phase. "Once I get to Chicago, Matt should be all ready to upload everything we recorded today. The formats are all set and, just in case, we have backup copies here in Portland," Mitch said. "The next challenge is going to be recording the acoustic basics for the other five tracks and then singing my ass off!" He paused. "And then racing a marathon."

Neil's response was straight and to the point. "You're gonna rock both!" Mitch smiled as he drew in a deep breath and gladly accepted his friend's vote of confidence.

"Drew," Mitch said. "I'm going to swing by your place tomorrow and grab your bass and analog synthesizer. Your keyboard is a Juno 6, right? Not that I'd know the difference in models, but I want to let Matt know what I'm bringing out. Are you around in the morning?"

"All morning!" Drew answered. "Come by for coffee!"

"Neil, can I please grab your drums on my way home from Drew's?" Mitch continued.

"What do you want to bring out there?" Neil asked.

"Your spare kick, snare, high hat, floor tom, kick pedal, and drum throne. Of course, I have no idea how these will sound out there, given that I'm not a drummer… But to just have them on hand and to be able to use the kit as a percussion instrument rather than as the backbone to a song would be super cool for spontaneity's sake."

Neil laughed, knowing that Mitch couldn't really play drums, but he had faith in the singer's creative process to make a really good CD. "My backup kit is all packed for you and ready for experimentation," the drummer replied.

The excitement with the work they had just completed seemed to have pressed Mitch's babble button. He was aware of this, but couldn't help himself from shutting up. "Guys, I so want to take you with me to record these other songs, but with three full band CD's already under our belts and three fourths of my shows being solo acoustic these days, my gut is telling me I need to make this record with more of an acoustic vibe." He paused and then added, "It's something I've always wanted to do, to really challenge myself musically… To give my songwriting a different recorded vibe and…"

Neil interrupted Mitch's soliloquy. "It's all good! You've paid for the last three CD's and put our names on each of them as an equal contributor. You're playing out solo more than ever and you ought to have a solo CD to sell. We've talked about this a bunch of times before."

"It's also going to be cool to see what you do with these tunes," Drew added. "Besides, solo road trips are always awesome! Especially when all you'll be doing is driving straight on a flat Interstate and thinking about the record's production."

"That, and how my body will react at the starting line of a marathon the day after the recording's completion!" Mitch interjected.

"Yeah, yeah," said Neil sarcastically. "Whatever."

Mitch returned the smile to each of them. "Thanks for being cool with this," he said to his friends.

Hugs given and a "see you tomorrow" statement shouted over their now running engines, each player stepped into their vehicles and drove away from the studio.

As Mitch hit the end of the block and made the first left on Cumberland Avenue, he did all he could do to resist the urge to listen to what they had just recorded. His ears were tired, his mind was numb, and as a perfectionist, he knew he'd notice something wrong with one of the tracks and would want to fix it. But what was recorded was the day's captured moment in time and could not be altered. *It is what it is,* he thought to himself as the smarter part of his brain won this particular battle. The sounds of the truck's engine and road noise instead, ensued.

He was going to miss his band during the upcoming creative process, but he also knew he was going to grow from making this CD alone and then following it up with what he hoped was going to be the race of his life. How he'd mature was yet to be determined. It was all a part of being a rock and roll runner.

Ghosts

T he highway stretched out for what seemed to be endless miles over the Ohio plain. The road's straight beauty bisected the adjacent fields of corn straight to the horizon. Above, the huge gray clouds expanded like giant butterfly balloons in the early morning sky as they scraped their wings together. Further enhancing the imagery of their well choreographed dance, the rising sun added her color.

Mitch inhaled deeply and took the first few strides of the day's short and easy taper run. The early fall morning's crisp taste gave him a sense of expectation, adventure, and optimism. He thought about how he had kissed Dylan goodbye twenty nine hours ago and was elated when she told him that she had bought a plane ticket to Chicago and would be there for the race. This added pledge of support again made him wonder how he had ever ended up being so lucky.

His next thoughts jumped to the day prior to his leaving, when he had first started packing for his trip. As he began to get his stuff together, his actions had felt similar to any of his previous journeys. However, as more gear had been staged in his basement to be loaded into his truck, it quickly became apparent that in order for him to remember to pack everything needed for both his recording and his race, he would need to embrace a split personality.

Since it would be the last thing unloaded when he reached Chicago, he had first packed his race day bag into the back of his truck. As he ran down the deserted Ohio road remembering the feelings he had gotten immediately after packing this first essential piece of gear, Mitch again began to feel nauseous from the nervous jitters of the huge race which was now within ten days. *I have no idea how my body is going to react*, the runner thought to himself. *I need to get over the fear. I'm gonna do great.*

He continued on at a jogger's pace as he went over the next things he had packed into his truck. Thinking about the drums he'd borrowed from Neil brought both pre-production ideas and doubt about how the record would turn out on the surface. He had never recorded a drum track in his life, which added to the negative what if's he felt about the upcoming sessions. *It's all* good, Mitch said to himself as he shook off any negative thoughts that flanked his mental defenses. Instead of fearing that he had possibly taken on too much at one time, he allowed himself to believe, *This is going to be the experience of a lifetime.*

Moving slowly down the road he couldn't help but laugh at his own fears as he replayed the mental ping-pong which occurred each time another bag or piece of music gear had been loaded into his pickup. *I knew I should have bought that shirt last* week, he said to himself as he imagined loading his gear while wearing a shirt that read, "I don't have A-D-D, I have... Look... Squirrel!"

Mitch then recounted the loading of his instruments, all eight of them. These were the last pieces of gear to be packed since they needed to be unloaded after yesterday's twelve-hour drive, which ended with pulling into last night's motel, the ever-present paranoia of instrument theft not letting him leave the guitars in his truck.

As the musician approached the one-mile mark of the morning's easy run, he replayed last night's scene in the motel lobby. *I knew it was going to happen, but the looks on all those people's faces as I brought in one guitar after the other...* Mitch said to himself. One by one, he had been asked by a different traveler where the show was, what kind of music he played, why so many guitars, and the inevitable, "I play! Let's get some beers and jam!" With an overloaded amount of uncertainty on his mind, he was a little sad with himself for turning down this gracious offer, thinking that maybe, in order to take his mind off of everything, that getting some beers and jamming wouldn't have been such a bad idea.

He knew that bringing all these instruments along and hauling them in and out of his truck would attract some attention. He also knew that having seven guitars and one bass might be a little overkill. But he also knew that, when building a song, each instrument has a place. For Mitch, it was better to have a large quiver of tones to choose from rather than just one instrument with which to try and cover all of the bases. The unwanted motel attention wasn't such a big deal. What ended up striking the runner in a humorous way was that after the trips back and forth to his truck, he had made another connection between running and creating music while locking up his truck for the night. *Just as a runner knows to mix up workouts, a recording artist knows to mix up tones.*

Negotiating his way around a pothole in the road, his mind began to digest the unexpected nostalgic feelings he had experienced while driving past his alma mater, the University at Albany. Though only a six hour drive from his home, Mitch had never felt the urge to visit. As his westbound travels to Chicago brought him by the campus, he couldn't help but reminisce over the four short years he had spent there. *It's so strange how big of an impact going to school there had on me,* he said to himself. *That was the last thing Dad said before leaving me alone in my freshman dorm room…* "Mitch, the next four years are going to define you as the person you will be for your whole life." *He was so right.*

The runner let his thoughts trail off into his past. He laughed to himself as he replayed the barrage of emotions that he'd felt while driving by the campus. Each revolution of his tires seemed to add to the bombardment of memories, which he hadn't thought about in twenty years. *Four years of memory packed into a thirty second drive past a school… Talk about déjà vu overload!* he thought.

Breaking the memories down as he ran, he thought about old girlfriends and one night stands, friends he had shared dorm rooms and apartments with, the bars, the constant roaming parties, his professors, his choice of classes, and the highly caffeinated all night study sessions. *And "The Exchange!"* he exclaimed to himself. *Starting that band was a huge part of me back then… And still is today,* he said to himself.

He thought about the time in his junior year when he went to rehearsal and played on acoustic guitar the first song he ever wrote, "Paintbox." He caught himself smiling as he relived the euphoria of hearing Dyer, Craig, and Larry bring his music to life as they spent the afternoon ironing out their arrangements and parts. *After that rehearsal, I was hooked,* he said to himself. *Mom and Dad sent me to college to get a business degree… Just one rehearsal of hearing a song that came from my heart being played by my band-mates and that's all it took to reset my priorities.*

Submerging himself in memories not thought about in years, each step he ran seemed to work as a form of therapy to connect the dots on how his life had progressed since that rehearsal. *I wrote two more songs for "The Exchange," we made our first demo, immature dreams of becoming famous caused me and Larry to fight over the band's direction, he quit, Johnny joined and pushed me to write more songs, we started doing a killer acoustic duo on the side, that got even more popular than the band, a manager with major label connections picked us up... And then I graduated.* He let this thought linger.

The runner felt his face tighten as he remembered what had happened next. *My parents were so kind to me,* he admitted to himself. *Mom getting me in on the ground floor at a Wall Street firm and Dad getting me hooked up with a paying function band... And the way I went around their backs to pursue my own music.*

To his own admission, he could have gone about things in a more mature way. However, he still would have made the same choice. *I was so not ready to do either of those things,* he said to himself. *And to then call my best friends in Albany who had just moved into my old apartment and to find out that a room was open because one of them had recently dropped out of school... It seemed like it was meant to be! I had to blow off the real world and go back to Albany,* he rationalized. *Johnny wanted to keep the duo going and all the people who loved to hear us sing were still there. It was my calling,* he confidently said to himself as he remembered the day his parents went to work in the morning, only to return later in the day to an empty bedroom and a note telling them what he had decided to do. *And if I didn't leave Long Island when I did, the move to Boulder never would have happened... Or Dylan.*

His mind went silent for a moment. His ears filled with the sounds of his footfalls and the subtle wind that just kicked up. *It's nutty how twenty one years later I'm still wrestling with the guilt that I let my folks down by not pursuing the path they had laid out for me,* he thought. *Driving by Albany yesterday really affected me in ways I didn't expect... I thought I beat all those ghosts years ago.* The runner continued to process his past.

Doing his best to again put his head space back into the positive, he said out loud, "I make music for a living, I get to race marathons, and I love my life." A few seconds later, his mind doubled down on his exclamation and said, *I made a quality-of-life decision back then. I chose music over the Manhattan corporate life. I'm not making the money that my degree would have gotten me, but I'm making enough... And that's just fine with me.*

He ran in silence for a few minutes as his mind, in snippets similar to a movie trailer, replayed his life's journey from his post-graduation return to Albany to present day. "Everything works itself out," was what involuntarily rolled off his lips. "One way or the other, it always does."

A crack of thunder in the distance quickly brought him back to the present. A minute later, a bolt of lightning shot across the vast horizon, its thunder resonating a few short seconds after that. As its echo receded, a crow landed on a stuffed dummy mounted in the middle of the cornfield to his right. Mitch looked into the field, and said, "Life's a crazy journey, Mr. Crow. Enjoy it!" Spooked by the runner, the bird left its roost and flew over him. It screeched and cawed at him in a way that almost said, "Tell me something I don't know!" The runner smiled.

He looked down at his watch. First glance quickly told him that his visit to the past had caused him to run further away from his motel than he had intended to. *Not good for my body,* he thought as he scolded himself for not adhering to the rules of the marathon taper, rules designed to keep the body limber in the days prior to the race without getting overworked. When he had set out this morning for what he considered to be a short and sweet run, he had accomplished the sweet, but his time out was definitely too long for what was supposed to be the mellowest time of his training.

Still, he rationalized to himself. *I made great time driving from Maine all the way to eastern Ohio... One day's drive. Today's drive to Chicago won't be nearly as long or hard.* As he did his about-face to return back to the motel to collect his belongings, he couldn't help but notice the voluminous source of the thunder and lightning. With no control over the circumstance, he accepted the inevitable wet running clothes he'd likely be wearing when he got back to the motel. *All a part of the adventure,* he thought as the cloud's first trickles graced his face.

Instead of running faster to get out of the storm, Mitch slowed his pace. He let the energy of the falling rain embrace him. For reasons he couldn't explain, he felt nurtured by the presence of the storm rather than threatened. As the precipitation went from drizzle to showers to rain to 'heavy at times,' the runner pushed on at a slow and consistent pace. He loved the emptiness of the farm road, the volume of the heavy rain's hard pitter patter as it engulfed the corn stalks, and the delicious earthy fragrance emitted by the freshly irrigated fields.

The rain soaked through his clothes. Each degree of moisture conjured up wonderful, nostalgic feelings of childhood as he actively sought out to splash in the larger puddles rather than avoid them. As he jumped from puddle to puddle, he asked himself how he could manipulate such unexpected joy into the upcoming week's recording session. *And how do I then carry this happiness over into running the race of my life?*

Puddles were now everywhere, splashed in the wake of each of the runner's jubilant footfalls. The temperature was perfectly balanced with the coldness of the rain. There was nothing uncomfortable about it. To Mitch, everything around him couldn't have been more perfect. He let all the good energy fill him to his soul's brim. "I'll figure it out," he said aloud. "But at this moment, I need to let now be now."

Twenty five minutes after his turn around, the rain let up. The runner left the cornfields behind and approached the Interstate's strip mall of motels and chain restaurants. Before making the left turn onto the busier highway, he stopped running, turned around to the rural expanse, and thanked the Universe for its inspiration.

While looking over the rain-soaked fields, a few clouds broke overhead. The split in the sky allowed a burst of sunlight to penetrate the large mid-western horizon. A gently curved rainbow quickly formed and illuminated over the landscape. The runner sat down and leaned his back against the stop sign on the farm road's junction. *If this is any omen on how next week is going to go for me, I'm pretty damned psyched!* he said to himself as the inevitable grin spread across his face.

Arrival

Some of the people wore running shoes. Others wore dress shoes to match their uniforms. A few others wore comfy sandals while random women wore stiletto heels. Though each person was uniquely dressed, they all wore the same similarly focused expression of heading to work. Today's expression, however, had a Friday vibe to it.

Mitch's early morning taper run cut through the collective energy of the downtown Chicago commute with feelings similar to a child's excitement after hearing the final bell on the last day of school. He was elated. Nothing could dampen his positive spirit. He knew he wasn't on the marathon's course, but he was near it. Every intersection he ran through displayed a billboard with an image of an elite or amateur runner. The photographed athletes each had a sharp look of determination on their faces. On the bottom of each sign, just underneath the bank's sponsorship logo, were random quotes of inspiration about why we run.

With the marathon just nine days away, the early morning commuters seemed to have expected folks like Mitch to be slaloming through them while they walked to work. Each oncoming person smiled and stepped aside to let the runner continue on his journey. As he made eye contact, he couldn't help but radiate back in their direction the overwhelming positive feelings he was experiencing. Though he was running slowly, he had the uncanny feeling that he was hovering over the sidewalks, the overpasses, the exhaust grates, and the city itself. He felt as if his running shoes were tickling the pavement the same way a migrating bird floats on the wind.

He had arrived in Chicago around four o'clock yesterday afternoon. Bypassing the downtown area in order to meet up with Matt and his assistant engineer, Ty, he had pulled his truck up to the front door of the studio, which was located on the outskirts of the west side of the city. *All right... This is where I'm going to spend the next eight days and nights*, the singer had thought after putting his truck in park. *What a cool place!*

The anticipated reunion between Mitch and Matt had gone as both had expected. An excited, but road weary musician pulled up to an urban building in front of a no parking sign, threw on his hazards, jumped out, hugged his friend Matt, and hugged Ty, even though they'd never met. The three immediately unloaded the instruments, amps, and drums up the two-story staircase to the loft studio. It had taken thirteen trips to unload everything while each took turns at watching the illegally parked vehicle and its beloved gear. Once the truck was empty and legally parked, Mitch's transition from the anticipation of what he had planned to do to the start of finally doing it had occurred.

It had been over four years since Mitch and Matt had worked together. But just like the way it should be with real friends, as soon as they reconnected, the two immediately clicked like a day hadn't gone by, now again side by side in a studio control room.

Talks of older projects between the two and how they would compare to the upcoming session had been the conversation's theme. As Mitch spoke and listened to what Matt had to say, he unpacked his guitars and placed each one on an individual stand around the studio. Even he had underestimated how excited he'd be about all of his guitars remaining within an arm's reach throughout the sessions. He was giddy.

"I think this is one of my favorite things about locking out a studio for a week," Mitch said as he sampled each guitar for the engineers. He excitedly noted to himself that he wouldn't have to pack any of them up until the recording was completed.

The runner stopped at a cross walk. *I'm so psyched to be back in the studio!* He looked left, noticed the less trafficked side street, and made the turn. Parked cars lined the left side of the street due to the alternate side parking ban signs. Mitch ran past them and the ten to twenty story residential buildings they abutted. With most of the apartments' occupants already at work, he was able to enjoy the mostly empty sidewalks. He let his mind wander as he continued to process yesterday's arrival.

"OK, where's the hard drive?" Matt had asked after the last guitar's sound had been sampled in the old brick environment of the newly converted studio. Mitch had reached into his backpack, pulled out the memory card, and handed it over to Matt to be uploaded to the studio's server. Mitch couldn't help but to hold his breath as Matt's software read and recognized the basics of the three songs, which Neil, Drew, and he had recorded in the Portland studio a week ago. *I'm so happy technology worked, and I didn't have to deal with overnighting another hard drive from Portland!*

Mitch left the sidewalk and ran in the street due to scaffolding on the building in repair in front of him. As he glided past the parked cars and replayed the scene of Matt and Ty listening to the three tracks for the first time, it occurred to him that, since his training had started, he looked at time differently. As a trained marathoner with a huge race only a few days away, everything in his mind was now measured by when he had completed his last long distance training run.

"I ran a really difficult twenty miler the week before we laid these tracks down," Mitch had said to no one in particular as the three listened to the tracks. The runner remembered catching eyes with the two of them, each holding a look that pondered why one would actually run that distance for fun and then race six miles longer just because. *Not surprising to see... They aren't runners.*

Passing a woman walking her five small dogs, Mitch said a soft "good morning." A few moments later, he laughed at the memory of rebutting Matt and Ty's perplexed look at his twenty miler statement. Rather than talk about the basics they had just listened to, during the silence in between the first and second song, Mitch instead had said, "There's a spiritual and physical beauty about marathoning. When you get to that really crazy endurance part of the training... You know, when running a seventeen mile run seems like you're just going out for a fun two and a half hours... It's like..." but the next song had started.

I gotta shut up with all the running stuff in the studio. I know it's on the forefront of my mind, but when I'm in recording mode, I need to mentally be there 100%, the runner said to himself as he continued down the street and made another turn onto a second side street.

He ran in silence for a bit, listening to the sounds of the city, the horns of the vehicles, the backup beeps of the reversing garbage trucks, the squealing brakes of the buses, a siren in the distance, and the eternal hum of the many buildings' air conditioners.

He stopped at a crosswalk and waited for the light to change. The last twenty seconds of "Move it Out" began to loop continuously in his mind. After the twelfth or thirteenth cycle, Mitch replayed how, last night, Matt had boosted his confidence right after listening to this track. "Love the vibe," Matt said. "This is gonna be a great session."

The light turned green in his direction. Mitch again started his mellow jog. With the motion of his legs causing his mind's cogs to turn, he recalled his conversation with the engineers regarding his vision and expectations of what he felt should happen over the next eight days. He had rehearsed this anticipated speech on his drive out to Chicago, knew it by heart, and had spoken to Matt and Ty with the same heartfelt passion one friend speaks to another when describing what they want to do with their lives. To Mitch's delight, both Matt and Ty had been psyched to hear what he had to say, before he even started.

"My goal is to make an eight song solo record. I've made three records with "Now is Now," each one I fully wrote and helped to produce. But this time around, I'd like to go for something different, something that reflects me as a solo performer, as an intimate singer/songwriter," Mitch began. As the two listened with open ears and open eyes, the singer had given his best. "I recorded these three tunes with Neil and Drew to give the record some versatility and some additional energy, aside from the fact that they're my best friends, and I want them on the record. These three tunes, I'm thinking, will be recorded the same way as I've done in the past: lay down a keeper guitar track to compliment the bass and drums, sing the lead tracks with doubling vocals and harmonies, and finish up the solos and textures at the end of the session."

Matt and Ty continued to listen without distraction.

"The other five tunes will be more experimental. I'd like the first recorded tracks for these songs to be the acoustic guitar. My gut is telling me that if I approach building the song around the acoustic guitar, instead of the bass and drums, there's a better chance of creating the singer/songwriter vibe I'm looking for." Matt nodded. Ty's eyes had begun to show some real excitement as Mitch rambled on. "Once the keeper acoustic tracks are down, I can then sing all the lead tracks, doubling vocals, and harmonies. Afterward, I'll add the backup guitars, keyboards, and drums.

At this point, Matt doubtfully chimed in. "How do you expect to lock up the drums to the guitars after the fact? I know you're going to play the keeper guitar tracks to a click track to keep your tempos consistent, but you know how hard it is to record the drums afterward." Mitch had let the engineer shed his thoughts, anticipating this reaction from him. "Drums are always recorded first. You know how sloppy a song sounds if the drums are recorded after the guitars," Matt finished.

Mitch's answer had been both immature and inspirational. "I'm not a drummer. Nor do I want to be one. But I'm really good at percussion and for some reason have an uncanny grasp of time and tempo." Matt nodded as he remembered this of Mitch from the last time the two worked together. "My goal is to play the drums like a big percussion instrument and to track the kick, snare, and cymbals by themselves so their tones are easy to isolate when I mess up. All my mistakes should be easy to re-do. We'll be able to punch in and minimize me having to start the song from the beginning each time I screw up."

The singer's rebuttal had made both Matt and Ty smile. Though Matt had been engineering for over twenty years and, during this time, had earned himself several Grammy awards, he'd never approached a project this way. For Matt, Mitch's passion to re-create the way to make his record had elicited a vote of confidence from the experienced engineer and the one word response: "Awesome!"

The runner hit another crosswalk and red light. He stopped his legs and slowed his mind. *I hope I know what I'm doing here. Matt is psyched with my proposed approach, loves the basics of first three tracks, and is certainly going to have an open mind to the recording of the others, but I need this to go smoothly.* The light turned green. Once again, he ran. *It's gotta go smoothly. My race... A smooth recording session will ensure I'm rested when I get to the starting line. A difficult recording session…* Mitch let this negative thought trail off.

He thought about how they had spent the next two hours listening to his pre-production tracks. Matt and Mitch were seated in comfortable swivel chairs while Ty stood ready to take notes at the studio's white board. Prior to hearing each song, Ty would write the title in the board's grid, underline it, and wait for Mitch's instruction. As they listened to each song, Mitch spoke about what he felt was needed to bring each song to life while Ty listed each comment underneath the song's title. *There was a lot written on that board after that exercise. I know we did that so the recording runs efficiently, but the overload look on Matt's face when we were done was a little intimidating.*

The runner continued on as he replayed Matt's reaction after listening to the eighth and final song and viewing all of Ty's notes on the white board. "Mitch, you've got a hell of a lot of work to do here, week's worth of work. How do you expect to make a great record in just eight days? You realize how exhausting all this will be." Mitch hadn't been able to keep himself from smiling through his pride. He had answered the only way he knew how. "I know how to push through difficult things and draw forth the positive," he said. "I'm a runner. We'll make it happen."

The three had let Mitch's response settle in as the sun disappeared beneath the skyscrapers of downtown. They shared a brief, awesome moment of silence as the soft lighting gave the studio a relaxed and blissful feel.

The runner made another turn, this time onto a much busier avenue. People were everywhere. He dodged commuters and workers loading goods down the steep steps of their storefront basements. Though the city's bustling energy surrounded him, the runner felt as if he were moving along in that same silence he had experienced after yesterday's conversation. *That was such a great feeling. I love connecting like that in the studio. It's good to be among friends.*

As a bus stopped in the crosswalk in front of him, its brakes let off a loud burst of compressed air. Pulling him out of his silence, the runner was reminded of how quickly yesterday's serenity in the studio had vaporized as Matt suddenly took over the reins. "Ty, food! Here's $50. Please go grab us a pizza with everything on it," he instructed. "And some IPA." Turning to Mitch he said, "The Chicago local brew is really nice." *Matt was certainly right about that.*

He next thought how Matt had quickly shifted gears, turned and faced the studio's console, and said, "I have about an hour left with a hip hop client's mix. Let me bang this out, we'll eat some good food, and then head back downtown to my place. You're really gonna dig it there. It's just a few blocks from the park where Obama spoke. I think that's where your race starts?" Mitch shrugged and admitted to Matt that, at that time, the only geography he knew about the city was the small studio room he currently occupied. "If you're not into listening to me work on this mix," Matt continued, "feel free to hang in the lounge or on the fire escape. It has great views of the downtown skyline."

With this said, Matt switched vibes as someone else's music took over the once silent room. With him at work and Ty gone for food and beer, Mitch explored the studio, eagerly looking for the fire escape and refuge from the hip hop.

He left Matt to his mix and found the fire escape door. He pushed open the door and let the unseasonably warm early October air brush against his face. *So surreal... It feels like summertime.*

Since arriving at the studio, the sky had slowly dimmed to dark blue. The artificial lighting from the streets and buildings played weak substitutes for the brilliance of the recent setting sun. Miles away, Chicago's tallest building and her concrete counterparts had become geometric silhouettes in the clear, darkening sky.

He climbed over the railing and onto the adjacent roof. He leaned back against a dormer and pondered all the excitement the upcoming week would bring. He'd thought these same thoughts on every long run over the past four months. However, while staring at the Chicago skyline, they held much more gravity. *Can I realistically take a project, which would likely take another player many weeks to complete, and do it inside eight days? Not just complete it, but execute it with what's needed to make the timeless recording I want to have for myself and my audiences. Could I inject 110% of my heart and soul into this project and still have enough energy reserves in my tank to race twenty six point two hard and fast miles the day after the session's completion?*

The memory stopped the runner in the middle of the sidewalk. He moved aside and let people pass him by. *All I can do is the best I can do. I said the same thing to myself last night while sitting on the roof and nothing has changed. I'm here, it's happening, and I'm just going to give it my all.*

He took a deep breath, checked his watch, saw that he'd been running for twenty minutes, turned, and jogged back in the opposite direction. A few moments later, he let himself pick up last night's memory, about a half hour into his solitude, when Ty opened the fire escape door to announce that there was food and had invited Mitch out of his meditation to gorge on greasy pizza while Matt finished up his mix.

In the control room, Matt had been going back and forth over a five-second section of the hip hop mix. The look on his face had been one of pure confusion. "Guys, listen to this lyric." When he pressed 'play' and the thump of the synthesized kick drum and bass filled the room, the song's rapper claimed that all the girls loved him because he "had good grapple." Matt hit the stop button and exclaimed, "What the hell is good grapple? Does this guy think his stuff is gonna sell with a lyric like that? I don't even know what grapple is, let alone good grapple. Jeez!"

While they drank their first beer, they searched online for the definition of grapple. They discovered it was a huge pole and hook tool which fishermen use to grab their catch. "I'm so glad this next week won't have lyrics like that one," Matt said. The three laughed hard as they created scenarios of a guy thinking he was cool by picking up girls in a bar using a grapple hook.

Now that's a much more fun memory to think about! More funny thoughts, less obsessing about running and recording!

With the pizza finished and a six pack of yummy beer gone, Mitch had looked up at the engineers and, again, got onto his soapbox. "Guys, I need to eat better than this. I'm not gonna stop you from eating an engineer's diet, but I'm running a nutty race next Sunday and I don't think grease is the best way to prep."

"How about sausage and peppers?" Matt asked. "Or BBQ chicken?" Ty interjected. "We've got an awesome soul food joint around the block!" The three laughed. Over the four years since his last recording, Mitch had forgotten that healthy food isn't a priority during recording binges. He had to be focused on staying healthy for the end of the week.

I know it was greasy, but the pizza is sitting pretty good in my belly right now, he thought as he made the turn off the avenue and onto the street with its looming scaffolding. *Maybe I can split the difference and eat a little of the nasty stuff they bring in?* He let this thought trail off as he crossed over to the other side of the street and its construction-free safety zone.

Another thing I forgot about with studio stuff was the timing of meals. If I'm going to spend twelve hours a day in a studio, I can't just go along with Matt and Ty and eat dinner at 10PM. The runner shook his head. He knew this would be a tough cycle to break, but if he was going to run a great race, it was a cycle that needed breaking. *My biorhythms need to be on and healthy if I'm going to manage my nutrition the right way for race day,* he thought, knowing that this was easier said than done.

Back on the main city street where he had started his run, he began to think about the healthier food he was going to buy at the supermarket on the way to the studio. A smile crept over his face as he replayed Matt's statement about trying not to brag too loudly about how good the fries were from the burger place just down the street from the studio. As the runner ran by a street-side diner, he thought, *I bet those fries smell as amazing as the bacon wafting out of this restaurant!* A few moments went by. He continued to jog down the block. The pungent aroma of delicious bacon hung in the air. *I gotta chill. I'll be healthy, but I'm going to have to eat some junk food if I'm going to make this experience fun.*

As he made up this last rule for himself, his early morning taper route brought him back to the downtown side street where Matt lived with his wife, Pam, and their three year old son, Carter. Mommy and son were playing with toy trucks on their second-floor patio when Mitch walked up.

"Uncle Mitch, play with me!" the toddler said. "I have big trucks!"

Pam smiled and said, "I think Mitch is here for other reasons than to play with you, Carter."

The runner laughed as he wiped the sweat from his brow and took in everything he had just pondered over the last forty minutes.

"I'm so psyched for everything to happen," he exclaimed to Pam with exuberance greater than her son's love for his big trucks.

The door then clicked open and Matt walked out to hugs from his family. He locked eyes with Mitch.

"Good run?" he asked.

"Couldn't ask for better," Mitch replied.

"Awesome!" Matt said. "Now go take a shower. Then we hit the studio and make a great record."

"I love the way you think!" Mitch answered as he smiled and walked up the stairs. His great week was just beginning.

Magic

The billboards around the city hadn't changed. The same people flooded over the morning sidewalk, consumed by thoughts of their upcoming work day. Downtown Chicago's Friday morning electricity was the same. But Mitch was different. He was running his last slow taper run over the identical city route he ran just a week ago. When he left Matt and Pam's apartment this morning, he had hoped to float with ease through the city streets. Sixty seconds into his run, however, the feelings in his legs made him think of an elephant's deliberate slog through a muddy drainage, thick with molasses-like sediment.

Last week's high-energy euphoria now felt soured with self doubt and the harsh understanding that he really did bite off more than he could chew. The reality that he might not be able to complete what he had started was now on the tip of his tongue. In short, he was beat.

With his marathon just two days away, he knew deep down that in order to race at his best ability, all he needed was just a really good night's sleep followed by a day of honest rest. Unfortunately for Mitch, there was no time for such indulgences. He was now just a day away from completing the recording of his new CD, an exercise which had required leveraging every source of energy within him.

He had spent the last four months driving all over northern New England, moving heavy gear, singing three-to-four-hour shows five to eight times a week, all on top of three core workouts of speed work, tempo runs, and long runs. He had chosen his gigging and training schedule, assuming - hoping - it would ready him for the week of making a CD and racing a fast marathon. To Mitch's disappointment, it now felt like the faults in his assumption would haunt him.

The runner slogged along the meandering streets, past the construction scaffolding, the woman walking her multiple dogs, and the many storefronts and markets. Twenty five minutes into his run, when he hit his turn-around point, he couldn't help but admit to himself that his body felt like he had been out for three hours and twenty five minutes.

Accepting this harsh reality, he stopped. He looked up past the skyscrapers and into the deep blue sky. Seconds later, he looked down at his running shoes. He came to terms with his error in judgment. Making a solo record was really hard, both mentally and physically. *And racing a marathon the day after I finish an eight day recording session is an absurdity!* he yelled at himself.

As he took the first slow steps back towards Matt and Pam's, he couldn't help but to reflect on the past seven days of recording. During the first day, it took some time to dial in the tones of his amp and choosing which guitar sounded best for the song in cue, but the day had seemed relatively easy. With the efficiency of a well oiled machine, he had recorded the basic rhythm guitar tracks for all eight songs. When he, Matt, and Ty had left the studio at eight o'clock that night, Mitch had assumed the remaining days of recording would be a cakewalk. *Nope...* he thought as he began to run. *Talk about being idealistic.*

But there was good reason to feel so optimistic about it all, another part of his mind retaliated. *Leaving the studio that night, I felt like I could conquer the world. It was so great!*

An involuntary smile crept over the runner's face as he thought about the sense of accomplishment he had experienced as Matt was locking the studio door that first night. It was delicious. For eleven straight hours, interrupted only by a lunch-break walk to a less-than-healthy burger joint, the day had been effortless.

The runner picked up his pace a little as he thought about how he had experimented with the tones of his guitar and, after some engineering brilliance from Matt, had recorded the most beautifully sounding guitar tracks of his career. By the time he had completed recording the foundation guitars for the CD's eighth song, he felt as if he had just cruised to a 5K PR. He was energized, elated, and psyched.

One hour later, over somewhat healthy pub salads and beer, the three sat in a micro brewery's booth and had decided the best route for the CD's recording was to next attack the more difficult phase of the recording: the vocals.

"I totally don't know what to expect," the singer admitted. "I've been confident this whole time, but now that the singing is about to start, I'm a little nervous."

"Even the greatest singers are nervous the day before they record," Matt replied as he locked eyes with Mitch and gave his best efforts to telepathically calm the singer.

"Yeah," said Mitch, "but those same singers have huge budgets and can re-sing their vocals again and again. What I lay down over the next week is what I live with… Forever."

"And that's the cool thing about this project!" interjected Ty. "The fact that this entire record is going to be a captured moment in time… Do you really want a CD of piece meal sessions which yield a vibe that's all over the place?"

"The continuity of this CD is what's going to be the best aspect of the recording," offered Matt. "Each song is going to have a psyched feel with the nervous anticipation of a huge race. By the way, I think you're nuts, but we can talk more about that later… Packing so much into such a short time will only help to give you the unique sound you're going for." After a sip of beer, Matt continued, "Don't think on it too much. Just sing like you have for the past ten years."

The next hour had been spent brainstorming how best to utilize their short amount of time in eliciting the best vocal performances Mitch could deliver without him blowing his voice out. Matt took out his laptop and opened a spreadsheet with each song listed.

"Alright, "Lyric of Life" first," he said to Mitch. "How many vocal tracks are we looking at?"

Mitch had spoken spontaneously, his mind's wheels turning as Matt tapped the ideas into his computer. "Lead vox, doubling vox for the choruses, two separate harmony tracks for the choruses, each with a doubled track, maybe a third harmony with a double… Likely a lead vox double on the pre-chorus. That's good for starters, I think?" The three continued like this as they hashed out what Mitch thought was necessary to make each of the eight songs great.

Man, it would have been amazing if recording the vocals were as easy as recording the guitars, Mitch thought as he continued on his return path towards the apartment. *Settling on mediocre vocal takes wasn't an option for me. I'm going to listen to this CD forever. There's no excuse for bad vocals. I want to listen to these songs years from now and be able to pat myself on the back and say "great job!"* The distraction of the memory had him absentmindedly slowing again as reality settled back into his legs. *But my best shot at perfection really took more energy out of me than I thought.*

The runner came to a crosswalk and stopped alongside several commuters waiting for the green light. As he stared past the 'Don't Walk' sign, he began to ponder the process of recording solid vocals. *Less is usually more,* he thought to himself, *but that's not always the case.*

The light turned green. He slogged across the street, just ahead of the commuters. *Eight songs... And I thought just eight easy lead vocal tracks and I'd be done. No... More like five hundred and eight with all the mistakes, doubling, and tripling... and then followed by four hundred and sixty four harmony attempts. That's a lot!*

When he went to the studio that second day, he knew he had wanted his recorded voice to sound amazing. But he also knew that in order to make this happen, he would need to take on the difficult task of first nailing each song's lead vocal and to then double parts of it. *When a song hits its climax, it's always better for the mix engineer to have more vocal tracks to work with,* he thought to himself as he ran. *Double or triple tracked vocals perfectly mixed together to make one great vocal take sound so good... And will often differentiate a good recording from a great one.*

Furthermore, he wanted it to seem like the songs on this CD were specifically written for each listener. *Each song should be a great production,* he thought. *And the perfect song always has great vocals... It's what everyone focuses on when they listen to a tune for the first time.* Mitch understood that recording a great song often took months to create, if everything went well. He knew this to be the norm in today's recording world. *And I took the genius stance and gave myself a week to do this. What was I thinking?*

Snapping the runner out of his thoughts, a runner coming at him from the opposite direction said, "Good luck Sunday!" as she approached him. He smiled, returned the gesture, and a few blocks later took a right turn towards the aroma of a strategically placed street vendor who beckoned him with a breakfast sandwich. Willpower winning out over bacon, the runner went back into his own world and further dissected the past week's studio experience.

Because Mitch knew recording vocals was the most difficult part of making a CD, after the first day of guitar basics, he had been the one to suggest starting the remaining sessions with recording both lead and harmony vocals. The plan was to limit Mitch's voice to three songs a day. *I thought I was being smart and avoiding stress by trying to get the best vocals down before time was running out and my race was quickly approaching,* he thought as he passed the food cart. *Man, did I have a reality check after that first day of singing!*

On day two, Matt and Mitch had met Ty at the studio around 10AM, each with morning coffee in hand and motivation in their eyes. During the first hour, Mitch warmed up his voice while he allowed his ego to convince himself that it would be a quick and easy day of singing. With his voice ready to sing and the limelight his and his alone, he had entered the vocal booth. Under the soft and relaxed lighting of the closet sized room, he saw that Matt had set up his favorite vocal recording mic, his friend Jon's AKG 414. After a quick sound check to make sure everything was working, Matt pressed the 'record' button for the first time that day.

The next few grueling hours had proceeded to whisk the singer back from his idealistic world with the shock of an unexpected kick to the stomach. *I sang so many shows over the past year... I still don't know why I find it so damned hard to make my voice sound good on tape,* he admitted to himself as he crossed another intersection.

Mitch slogged on. He came to the turn which brought him by the construction scaffolding. He crossed over to the safer side of the street. *By the time I finished singing the lead vocal for* "Middle," (*I think at three o'clock?*) *reality had kicked my ass.* He remembered sitting behind the studio console and calculating the time it would take him to track the lead vocal doubles, harmonies, harmony doubles, and to then do the same for seven more songs. *I didn't think I'd be able to finish all the tunes,* he thought as he made a turn onto another residential city block.

"That's when I had my first real freak out," the runner said out loud as he thought about how he had had a sudden need get the hell out of the mood controlled air conditioned environment of the studio and into some fresh air. He needed to re-think how to approach his vocals.

He recalled opening the fire-escape door and experiencing an irony he wasn't prepared for. The air outside the studio had been similar to the heat he was running in today: eighty hot, humid, and sticky degrees. Fears of how to flawlessly sing an exorbitant amount of vocal tracks had quickly been replaced by fears of a hot and sticky race. The anxiety of a possible heat infused breakdown twenty or so miles into his marathon affected the singer so negatively that he had to literally slap himself back to what he was doing.

This is my moment in time! I'll be listening to this CD for years. My friends and fans will hopefully want to listen to this for years as well. I need to find my groove and nail these tracks... It's now or never.

Over the next four and a half hours, Mitch would sing, listen, sing, get some air, listen, pound water, sing, listen, take an ear break, and do it all over again. By the time he exhausted his voice and could no longer deliver a quality vocal take, he had recorded all the lead and harmony vocals for two songs. It had been 7:30 when the second song was finished. Though he had been behind in his aggressive vocal schedule, he at least felt a sense of accomplishment in singing both songs well. Moreover, he had been psyched the second song took much shorter to complete than the first.

The runner turned onto a major avenue. *I completely underestimated how hard it was to record my voice. I knew it wouldn't be easy, but it took more energy and focus than I had planned.* A deeper voice from somewhere else in his brain then piped in. *Just like you always forget how hard a marathon can be. Remember the fun you had from three hours on during your last race?* Mitch had to smile sarcastically to himself and then tell himself to shut up.

As he ran alongside the morning commuters, his thoughts drifted back to the waning hours of the first day of singing and the moment when he had finished recording and listening to the day's second song, "Lyric of Life." "What do you think, no more vocals for the day and instead lay down some bass and percussion?" Matt had asked, followed by, "it is dark out."

When Mitch opened his mouth to answer, Matt interrupted. "That wasn't a question, Mitch. That was a statement. You're going to rest your voice. It doesn't matter that you're one song behind in your vocal schedule. You're going to lay down some bass and percussion tracks. We're only going to work for a few more hours. After, we're going to eat a huge dinner, and then you're going to go to sleep," he continued. "You just sang your ass off, and you have a hell of a lot more singing left to do. As you manage the CD's production and progress, I need to manage your energy level."

Mitch smiled and looked at Matt. "Why, because I almost fell over after singing that last chorus?" he answered while shaking his head. "It felt like a slap in the face when I thought I had just sung the best vocal take of the day and you wasted no time in telling me that the first line was good and the second line was flat and that I would need to sing the whole chorus again." He paused and took another deep breath. "Recording the bass line for "Lyric" and a few shakers and tambourines for "Middle" is a fine idea," followed by, "And then let's get the hell out of here and eat!"

Running his slow pace back toward Matt's apartment, a smile broke across his face as he again acknowledged for what seemed the hundredth time that week: the amazing benefit of choosing to record with a good friend who truly cared about his CD's outcome. *Taking the vocal mic away from me when he did likely saved my voice for the rest of the session. And he had to do that each day! That totally helped with the CD's good vibe.* He paused for a second in his thoughts... *Yet another thing to be extremely thankful for.*

A music producer's job is to be the ears of the listener. Whether the listener hears a song for the first time or has been listening for years and can't get enough, the music needs to be timeless and great. To accomplish this when recording, one's ears need be rested, sharp, and stay that way throughout a long session. However, after hearing the same song over and over played back in headphones while singing and re-singing vocals until they're perfect, it's extremely difficult to separate oneself from the song and to listen to it like you're hearing it for the first time. Mitch often equated this feeling to burning his mouth on a hot piece of pizza. After that first bite, he wasn't able to taste the rest of the slice. In short, after recording so many vocals, his ears were numb.

As this reality set in, Mitch had let go of his control over the recording's production and instead, focused on being psyched about choosing to work with Matt. As the days ground on, it had become obvious to Mitch that, as his production skills waned, Matt would pick up the slack. *There was no way Matt was going to let a bad vocal track be on this CD*, he thought as several other runners coincidentally turned off a side street and ran next to him.

"Racing Sunday?" a runner asked him.

"Oh yeah!" Mitch answered, "You guys?"

"I've got a friend who's running," said a runner. "No way can I run that far," said another, followed by a third runner, "It's awesome you can train your body to do such a cool thing."

"Which is likely why I feel like such a slug right now!" answered Mitch through his smile.

"But you're supposed to run slow," said the first runner. "At least that's what my friend says about running the week before a marathon... So you can show up at the starting line rested?"

"Well," said Mitch. "That's the plan. My fingers and toes are crossed."

"You going for a specific time?" asked another runner.

"I'd like to PR," said Mitch. "I ran a 3:27 in New York last year and it would be so cool to beat that."

"Is that under an eight minute mile pace?" asked the second runner.

"Yeah," answered Mitch. "As tired as I feel right now, it seems ridiculous that I'm even telling you guys."

"You'll do fine," said the first runner. "All you marathoners get nervous and tired right before the big day. And then you're on the starting line and something awakens in you… And then you kick ass!"

Mitch's gaze held the other runner's eyes as he processed this last statement. "Magic *does* happen on race day, doesn't it…" Mitch said.

"Sure does," said the runner. "Every time."

They ran together in silence for a minute, maybe two. Mitch couldn't tell. He was so unexpectedly happy to be sharing the last few of his pre-race miles with other runners that he couldn't help but to pick up his pace to match theirs… And it felt good!

"We're headed left and back to our office to start our work day," one runner said after a few blocks had passed. "Good luck Sunday!" said another runner. "Kick ass!" said another. "Such an awesome thing you're about to do," said a third. "Have a blast running with fifty thousand runners!" said the first runner.

Mitch thanked them as they turned and left him running straight on the busier avenue. *What an awesome group of folks to spontaneously meet*, he thought. After replaying the brief conversation he had just had, he repeated to himself, *Magic always happens on race day*. Taking pride in the positivity which he defined himself by, the runner made the conscious choice to smile. *I've experienced the magic before, and I'm going to experience it again. I'm trained. I'm ready, and it's all good.*

For the same unknown reasons why endurance runners often find strength after admitting to themselves that they have none left, his tired mind recalibrated and woke up. *I GOT THIS!* he yelled at himself as he pushed his legs a little bit harder. His slightly faster pace seemed to open his heart. He thought about the movie *Forrest Gump* and the scene when Forrest ran away from his bully classmates as hard as he could, shattering his restrictive leg braces in his sprint as his friend Jenny screamed "Run, Forrest, Run!!!" He picked up his pace a little bit more. He embraced the feeling of rising above his creative exhaustion. For the first time since his initial and tiring day of recording vocals, he felt like a runner.

You did good! he said to himself as he cruised across another intersection. *I'm picking the whole recording experience apart. Stop. Matt and Ty both said at the end of yesterday's session that the entire week had been a great experience and the CD was sounding fantastic.* Positivity now firmly in place, he repeated, *Mitch, you did good!*

Endorphins flowed and swirled in his blood the way sweet vanilla and chocolate flowed out of a soft serve ice cream machine into a cone. He focused on additional positive happenings from the past week. He first replayed the conversation he had had with one of Matt's hip hop clients, a full bodied and big man who had come into the studio to pick up a mix. Upon chatting with Mitch about his CD and his upcoming race, he dropped his jaw on the mixing console when Mitch showed him the map of the marathon course. "You're running all the way up there?" he had said. "I don't even drive up there!"

And when I finished singing "Old Habits…" *That totally touched me,* he said to himself as he remembered the look on Matt's face when he came out of the vocal booth. "Mitch, we've made two other records together and on each one, you made me cry," Matt had said after locking eyes with Mitch. "Damn, you did it again… That's a great song, Mitch!"

His smile continued to widen as he next remembered how in the last hour of yesterday's session, when he had played drums for the last track of "Replace." Upon finishing the tune, both Matt and Ty had remarked that with huge drums as the song's backbone, this song, which during the six previous days had been their least liked, had suddenly become their favorite.

And then Matt this morning… What a trip! he said to himself as his smile became sprinkled with drops of laughter. *All those nights of him eating like shit just to spite me finally caught up with him.* Three days ago, Mitch had drawn the diet line with Matt and Ty and had made salads for lunch and pasta for dinner each day. Each time he ate his race building vegetables and carbs, the two engineers would indulge on sausage and pepper sandwiches. Last night, Matt had upped his ante and had eaten two greasy extra spicy subs for dinner. While trying to fall asleep last night, he had battled some awful stomach gas and severe indigestion. "I thought I was having a heart attack," he had told Mitch this morning. "I even got out of bed to Google 'heart attack symptoms.' But after reading them, I decided that my thirty five year old body was OK because I didn't feel symptom number seven, the feeling of impending doom."

This morning, before his run, Mitch had found no humor in this. He had his own feelings of impending doom. But after chatting with the other runners and flipping his perspective around, he now had to stop running because he was laughing so hard.

As his laughter tapered to a giggle, he began to jog. *I'm back! But take it slow…. I've got a race in forty eight hours. And first, I have my last day of recording in front of me.* He itemized the remaining tracks he'd need to record in order to finish the CD. Taking only a few moments to complete this task, his next inspiring thought was, *I'm done singing vocals, I'll be touching up a few loose ends on all the songs, and by tomorrow afternoon, Matt, Ty, and I will likely be sitting in front of some really loud speakers having a listening party.*

The runner again, stopped. He put his hands on his hips, held his head high, and said out loud, "And then we burn a rough mix for me to listen to all the way home to Maine!" Before taking his next step forward, he exclaimed through his smile, "I did it!"

He made the final turn off the avenue and onto Matt and Pam's street. A few buildings before the apartment, he slowed to a walk, patted himself on the shoulder for completing four months of hard training, and sighed a huge expanse of air.

Slowly walking towards the building's staircase, he took inventory of his body. His next thought was how his trained body compared to everyone else who would be lining up with him on Sunday. *I'm likely in the same boat as the majority of racers. I don't think that most of the runners worked their asses off this week the way that I did, but I'm sure everyone is feeling nervous and tired in some way... Nervous about the unknowns of what we'll all feel like at the starting line, as well as what we'll all feel like at the twenty mile mark.*

His mind wandered as he did his best to mentally connect with the fifty thousand other runners who were likely stressing about the same thing. *And I bet each runner feels as beat as me... The single moms, the single dads, the married moms and dads, the teachers, the forest rangers, the sales people, the restaurant workers, the lawyers, the doctors... I bet there were several times when everyone's training plan said "run twenty miles" and life happened and got in the way*, he rationalized. *I can't be the only one who went through that. But we each found the time and energy to get out and run the required twenty. We're all the same. We all trained hard. We finished the four month journey. The race is here, and now we're all psyched!*

The runner continued his internal soliloquy. *We sign up for these races for a million different reasons, but at the root of it all, we sign up because we're all super heroes. We're goal oriented. We like to push our bodies to limits greater than the average person, and we all want to smash our goals. We're marathoners.*

As he walked up the stairs to the outside patio where Pam and Carter would likely be playing, he finally balanced reality with his positivity. *I know my exhaustion might keep my race pace back a bit, but my body has surprised me before. I just gotta wait and see what race day brings. Next steps, finish the CD, rest as much as I can, kiss Dylan like crazy when she gets here tomorrow night, and then kick ass on Sunday!*

Matt heard Mitch climbing the stairs and met him halfway up.

"How's the belly?" Mitch asked.

"Not needing anymore sausage! Damn, that was a weird experience!" Matt said over Mitch's laughter, followed by, "Wow, you're a different person than you were an hour ago. What gives?"

"Magic. Hopeful magic, Matty," he said as he looked into his friend's eyes. He next placed his hand on Matt's shoulder, walked past him, and up the apartment stairs to shower, change, and leave for the studio one last time.

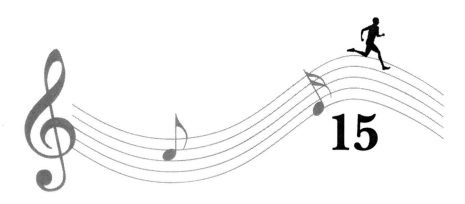

Turning Point

"Do you want to listen to my new CD again?"

"Don't you have something else you should be thinking about?" Dylan responded as she turned from the alarm clock, shook her head and smiled. She was standing across the room by the now silent alarm. "You had to set four alarm clocks?"

"What if the other three alarms didn't go off?" Mitch countered.

She walked back to the bed and sat down next to him. "Good morning," she said, and then leaned in to kiss him. After their kiss, Mitch stared at her. *So beautifully alive and awake,* he thought to himself. *How does she do that?*

"You need to *not* be thinking about your CD and get your thoughts on running, Mister!" she said to him.

"I know… I was just teasing," he answered while admitting to himself that if Dylan had answered "yes," he wouldn't have hesitated to press the 'play' button on the CD player.

Mitch looked across the room. The clock read 4:04 AM. His next glance was at the floor next to the bed. His race clothes were all laid out and waiting. He next looked into the corner where his post-race clothes were packed in his finisher bag. Adjacent to the bag was a permanent magic marker to mark his arm with his hopeful pace times. Next to the sharpie was his race belt which held his electrolyte gels. Perched on top of his finisher bag was his fleece jacket and running cap. His running shoes waited beside the small pile.

The runner looked back at his wife. Besides the happiness she gave him by simply showing up for his race, he felt an enormous amount of love and gratitude. He thought about last night and the way she had helped him shed his pre-race nervous energy. He had loved watching her pin his race bib on his shirt and then use her perfect penmanship to write MITCH just over his number. After his race stuff was laid out on the floor and his post-race stuff was packed, she had helped him calculate realistic pace times, offered advice on the smartest way to run the race in the forecasted hot sun, when to hydrate, when to eat his electrolyte gels, and when to push hard.

She had also switched gears for him. Soon after the last of her running advice was given, she had put on a pair of headphones and listened to the rough mixes of his new CD. To Mitch's delight, she sang along to each song and smiled when he had hoped she would.

Mitch's glance returned from his running stuff and again held her eyes.

"What?" she asked.

"Everything!" he said back to her.

"Don't get all mushy on me now," she answered. "You need to focus on the super fun day you have ahead of you. I'll get started on coffee!" As quick as that, she was out the bedroom door, leaving Mitch to wake up in his slow and deliberate way.

As if in a trance, the runner stared blankly after her. Her last comment turned his mind and emotions towards the huge day in front of him. Newly hatched butterflies in his belly quickly made him aware of how nervous he was about racing marathons. *I'll never get over the pre-race jitters*, he thought. *I think it's safe to assume that most of the people running today are probably feeling the same way.*

He thought about the millions of people around the world who race the distance every year. The sport had become so popular that running a marathon started to feel commonplace… Almost. *But there's a huge difference between running a marathon and racing one,* he said to himself.

Though he had three marathons under his belt, he had only raced his previous one. This experience was completely different from his first two. During his third and fastest marathon, when he had pushed his body through the late miles in the race, he had learned that something unique and awful occurred… *Right around the twenty mile mark.* He did his best to try and remember what this late-in-the-race feeling was like so he would know how to overcome the doubt, pain, and negativity, which such an effort inevitably brings. *If I'm going to race this thing and go for a PR, it's gonna hurt. I'm gonna feel like shit, and I'm gonna wanna quit. When this happens – and it's going to happen – I need to make the right choice between run or quit… I gotta keep running, no matter what.*

He next thought about last night's coaching conversations he had had with Dylan. One particular statement seemed to weigh heavier than the rest. "If it's a hot day, you'll need to adjust your goal to a slower pace or you'll likely completely fall apart," she said. Mitch rolled this possibility around in his head.

His restless mind then jumped to the memory of his reunion with Dylan at 7PM last night. His phone had lit up with the text "I'm here!" and within seconds, he was out of the apartment door and jogging to the bus stop. As happy as he was when running towards her, he couldn't help but feel concerned about the city's night time temperature. *So what, the sun was down and it felt like I was running towards the ocean for a summertime night swim instead of running towards Dylan in the middle of October,* he thought.

But the jog had been short and the kiss with Dylan long. His concern had been short lived. With Dylan's immediate absence in the bedroom, however, the bliss he had felt while around his wife had suddenly worn off. His camouflaged fears came out of hiding and resonated throughout his body. *I've stressed a lot about a possible really hot race day over the past week. I thought I was over this. Regardless of what race day brings, I'm going to race hard and do the best that I can.* But now that he was alone, a little after 4AM, in a strange bed, in a distant city, with an epic day in front of him, his anxiety flowered. Negative emotions seemed to overwhelm him like a swarm of hungry mosquitoes.

"Stop!" he said aloud. "It's just a race. There's no need to stress about it like this. It is what it is!" The runner did his best to convince himself of this. But deep in his heart, where he was the most honest he could be with himself, he knew it was more. Today's race was a turning point in his running career. It was a turning point which every lover of fitness experiences at some point in their active lives.

Over the last eight years, he had spent much of his downtime tuning his body. Every time he signed up for another race, whether a 5K, 10K, 25K trail race, ½ marathon, or marathon, he'd force himself to train harder and smarter. Finish line after finish line, he would hit a personal record, regardless of the race's distance or the conditions he had run in.

His first marathon, five years ago, was an experiment to him. His goal, to simply finish running twenty-six-point-two miles, was an enormous undertaking for him. *Finishing that race in 4:17 wasn't fast, but being my first marathon, it was a PR,* he thought to himself. For his second marathon, run three years ago, he finished in 3:56. *I wasn't properly trained for that race,* he rationalized. *I was singing four nights a week and working my forty-five-hour-a-week day gig… I put a lot of training time in, but not enough.* His third marathon, run eleven months ago… 3:27, a personal record and amongst the top fifteen percent of the forty five thousand finishers. *And I ended up in the medical tent with dehydration and muscle spasms,* he remembered. *I just don't know if I have any more to give than when I ran that day. How can I beat that time?* He let this statement sit for a few moments. *Music was my only job, I trained hard, trained smart, read all about the right way to race the distance, and gave it my all. How can I manage to give more?*

The runner shut his eyes and took a deep breath. As he thought about his prior races and how he had become faster and faster, he had also noticed that his PR's were no longer set by large chunks of time. *They're set by minutes, even seconds,* he said to himself. *I wonder if my forty one year old body is finally hitting that point. What did I call it again? My genetic threshold... Quite a silly, made-up, scientific term,* he thought. *But I think it's really happening. What if last year's marathon was the fastest my body could run, regardless of how hard I trained for today's race?*

From his training's outset, he did his best to convince himself that what he was about to undertake was going to be his fastest marathon. He trained harder than he ever had and completed each of his long training runs with both a strong finish and a visual manifestation of a finish line clock reading five to ten minutes faster that his NY time.

Again, he thought about last night's jog towards Dylan and how hot it had been. Gut feelings of having a bad day wouldn't leave his scattered brain. *Racing a marathon in summer conditions is not my thing, especially after putting in as many hours in the studio as I did this past week,* he thought. *Even if I was rested, high temperatures would still kick my ass. And I'm going to be starting this thing already tired.* Again, he let this thought sit for a few moments. *What the hell did I get myself into?*

Mitch opened his eyes. He took another deep breath. He swung his legs over the side of the bed and walked towards the bathroom. He switched on the light and took a long hard look into the mirror. *This is going to be hard. I might not be as fast as I want, but happiness is mine to choose,* he said to himself as his eyes locked with the mirror's reflection. *My mantra has saved me before, and I'm going to have to call on it to save me again.* For what seemed like the gazillionth time that week, he again said out loud, "It is what it is, and I'm gonna do the best I can." He then added, "And it's my choice as to how I'm going to deal with what's presented to me."

As he let the sound of his voice fade in the small bathroom, he took another hard look in the mirror. The street light outside of the window gave a glancing touch of gold to the runner's aura. *I'm still me. Regardless of the weather, I'm gonna do my best to kick ass. It might be hot, but I won't know what the heat will do to me until I'm well into the race,* he said to himself. *And there's no way of knowing unless I go for it.*

After brushing his teeth and washing his face, Mitch gave his reflection one last stern, strong, and focused look. "You got this!" he said out loud to his reflection. He turned, walked back to the bedroom, dressed in his race uniform, picked up the rest of his gear, and skipped down the stairs towards the aroma of magic coffee beans. *And there's a princess preparing the perfect mug for me,* he happily thought.

"There you are!" Dylan said as he entered the kitchen. With a half finished mug in one hand, she offered a second full cup of elixir to Mitch with the other. "I was beginning to wonder if you had decided to go back to sleep," she said through her smile.

He took the mug, sipped it gingerly, and said a heartfelt "Thanks."

"You're welcome," she replied.

"No," Mitch said, "Thanks for loving me. There's way too much going on in my head right now. I don't know how I'd be dealing without you."

"Well, you don't have to think about that, do you?" she responded as she uncapped the sharpie.

She took Mitch's forearm. So the runner didn't have to do the time versus mileage math in his head while racing so many miles, he wanted her to write on his forearm the six pace times that he considered important to hitting his goal finish time. She spoke softly, almost to herself as she did this, noting the mile markers first, "Mile five, ten, thirteen point one, sixteen, twenty, twenty three."

Mile markers now a dark black scribble on his white wrist, she looked at him and asked, "Do you want me to correspond these mile markers with the 3:20 or 3:30 finish times?"

"3:20" said Mitch without hesitation, as he latched onto the resilient imagery of the finish clock he had been imagining for the last four months.

"Nice!" Dylan said as she tickled his forearm with the permanent marker, "You're going for it."

"I'm a runner," was his next offering to the conversation. "I got this!"

"Well, let's go then!" Dylan answered.

They put their empty mugs in the sink. Dylan grabbed the filled travel mugs of coffee and bagels she had toasted and buttered while Mitch debated his race day approach. Not knowing if he needed it or not, Mitch pulled on his fleece. As his head came through the hole in the top of the garment, he took a breath and muttered to himself, *I really hope this fleece is necessary.*

The two opened the door of the apartment and took their bagel bowls and travel mugs down the block, across the street, and over to the sheltered bus stop. As they walked, Mitch was pleasantly surprised to have noticed that the temperature had dropped a little overnight. The fact that he actually needed his fleece briefly elated him.

They arrived at the bus shelter and quietly ate their breakfast. "Do you feel that?" Mitch rhetorically asked as the first of the day's warm breezes began to mingle with the cool dawn air. The soft, warm wind meandered around their existence with the heaviness of an impending battle.

As Mitch sipped his coffee, he made the choice not to dwell on what he couldn't control. He broke the gravity of their silent thoughts by itemizing what he had eaten the previous day. "If calories are what are needed to get me through this race, I sure have a lot of them in me!" He said.

After hearing Mitch's menu from the previous day, Dylan said, "A gallon of electrolyte drinks, sixteen ounces of pasta, an overloaded BLT, plus all the other stuff you noshed on… All eaten yesterday. Yeah, you're good to go in the heat. No worries." As she said this, she caught Mitch's eye. She next shrugged her shoulders. "I think?" was what next came out of her mouth with a sarcastic and humorous inflection.

The two loved their time together while waiting for the bus. They giggled with each other as Mitch told her funny stories from the week spent recording the CD. The sound of their murmured laughter on such an early, quiet morning elicited a random feeling of déjà-vu from Mitch's childhood; he felt like he was at a sleep-over party with his elementary school friends, a party where, after you went to bed, you weren't allowed to laugh too loud or a parent would come in and yell at you. But you laughed anyway. These memories added to his good feelings.

They finished their bagels and continued to drink their coffee. As they drank, a few other runners and their respective support teams joined them in the shelter. "Good mornings" were passed between the groups. Each runner couldn't help but to look the other runners over. As they waited for the downtown bus to arrive, sounds of sighs, crunches, sips, muted conversation, and the constant crinkle of gear bags emanated from the shelter as each runner repeatedly checked and re-checked that what they had in their bags was what they needed.

Mitch finished his coffee, put his cup in Dylan's bag, and looked at the groups around him. He began to realize that the collective energy of the race's anticipation was thrust upon him. He again nervously went through his gear bag. While doing this, he noticed himself becoming elated as he realized that this was the start of the big race experience. *It's super early, Sunday morning, dark, and the only folks on the streets are runners and the families of runners. Only a marathon creates scenarios like this.*

As the arriving bus headed towards the bus stop, each runner took their hands out of their gear bags and tightened their bag's drawstrings. The bus came to a halt in front of them. The doors opened as the bus's compressor gave out a harsh burst of steam. One by one, the runners and their families and friends boarded the bus. Mitch and Dylan were the last group to board. While walking down the dark aisle to find seats, Mitch made eye contact with the uptown runners who were already on the bus. Though each athlete was lost in their own thoughts and mental checklists, it seemed they all simultaneously loved the camaraderie of being a marathoner. Smiles, nods, and "Good Mornings" were given by everyone Mitch made eye contact with.

They rode the bus for five minutes. As they approached downtown, Mitch became focused on the intersecting streets, flush with endless lines of buses, cabs, and cars dropping off runners. So many people headed towards one central place from so many directions made each downtown street mimic a primary vein, which channeled the blood of countless runners towards the city's athletic heart.

The bus door opened and the athletes and their support teams got off. Stepping onto the pavement, Mitch noticed how quickly he became engulfed by the throngs of runners. It was difficult for him to absorb, but the scene nonetheless made him involuntarily smile. *Just thirty minutes ago, Dylan and I were two giggling love bugs eating breakfast in a bus shelter. And now, within minutes, the morning turned and multiplied itself into fifty thousand athletes heading towards fifty thousand life-changing experiences.*

Mitch had trained for months, mostly alone. He had run several shorter races to help prepare, yet those races capped out at a few thousand athletes, if that many. Today, among thousands and thousands of his fellow runners, each with the same nervous smile on their face and passionate focus in their eyes, he couldn't help but feel the true amazement of being a part of the electrical presence created by a city of runners about to race a marathon. *Not just a marathon, but the Chicago Marathon,* he said to himself.

"Look at everybody," Mitch said. "This is awesome!"

Dylan took hold of his hand. The runner gripped back, felt his love flow from his heart to hers. He pushed away all thoughts of race-day worry and embraced his positive. "This is gonna be so much fun!"

Choice

T he group of runners made their way past the fifteen mile marker. They ran in silence. Sounds they heard were the slaps of the footfalls of other runners, the labored breathing of runners who went out too fast, and the few cheering spectators who had gathered on the outskirts of the city. They were at the point in the marathon where the excitement of running a huge race in a beautiful city was beginning to wane.

"Great job! Keep it up!" yelled a man on a bicycle who was riding along side of the course. The runners didn't know who he was talking to. They kept their eyes pointed forward and their focus on the next eleven point two miles ahead of them.

"I can't do this anymore!" a woman in the middle of the pack suddenly exclaimed to no one in particular.

"You look great, honey!" the cyclist continued, his comments now obvious for who his cheers were for.

The woman looked in the direction of the bicycle as she began to slow her pace. She said in a harsh and discernible tone, "That's easy for you to say! You've got wheels underneath you!" The man on the bike had no response.

The other runners tried to ignore the domestic dispute around them. A few seconds passed. The woman looked to her feet and said aloud to herself as she slowed to a walk, "I'm done." Just like that, she stopped running.

The pack of runners around her kept silent as they ran passed her. To the group, it seemed that when she let everyone know she was quitting, it was as if her voice created a vacuum which sucked all the life out of the running experience.

At this point in the race, things began to feel surreal to Mitch. Just after passing the now idle woman, he looked down at his watch. He and the group around him had been running for a little over an hour and fifty minutes. Their average pace hovered around a 7:35 mile. He made eye contact with a few runners around him. Without a word being spoken, thoughts were exchanged between them. *Her quitting early wasn't a good omen*, they seemed to say each other.

The course had brought them away from the downtown area and onto a city block lined with short three to six story apartment buildings. The unseasonably hot sun had just crested over the rooftops. Mitch looked up at the tops of the buildings. He quickly noticed the hot air's shimmering effect off the reflecting roofs. *There's an image that only a lazy summertime sunbather could love*, he said to himself.

They continued to run in silence. To Mitch, it was as if the sun was acting like a golden sponge sucking the valuable moisture out of everyone's bodies. *Like the quicker picker upper*, he muttered to himself as the image of a long ago paper towel commercial, the one which showed how well a brand of paper towel sucked the spilled water off the table with quickness and ease, unintentionally entered his thoughts. *The sun is doing the same thing.*

I can't go there, he said to himself. *So what, a runner quit… And it's so much hotter than we all expected. I have eleven miles to go. I gotta keep the positive dominant if I'm gonna keep this pace up.* He thought about how he was going to do this. *Think about how happy you were just a couple of hours ago*, he told himself. *Hold onto that!*

The runner forced his mind to travel back to when the race's starting horn blew. It had been hard for him to accept the greatness of fifty thousand runners moving in the same direction at the same time. *It took me over five minutes to cross the starting line because of the thousands lined up in front of me. Man, that was hard for me to comprehend, but not hard for me to smile at,* he said to himself.

What was even more euphoric to him was when he had finally crossed the giant "START" painted across the city street and began to run. Each athlete, who just a moment before the horn had sounded, had been shaking off their nervous jitters in their own way. *We all shared the same nerve-racking feelings,* he said to himself. *But when it was finally time for us to run, it seemed like we were floating. Nothing else mattered. All fears vanished and happiness took over. Only the marathon does that to runners.*

Though he had studied the course's route hundreds of times before race day, Mitch couldn't help but feel lost in the twist and turns he had followed during the early miles of the race. He had felt as if he were being pushed along in a wave of quick runners around the city's streets. The current had taken him through an unexpected tunnel, out into the daylight and the shadows of the monolith skyscrapers, and finally, out onto the open arteries which delivered the masses to and from the downtown area.

He remembered jumping behind a shorter, fit woman who had written on the back of her shirt, "wanted: a fast man who dares to keep up with me." A little while on, another woman, this one tall and trailing long brunette braids, had past him with the grace and ease of a trotting thoroughbred. Written on her back was "you've just been passed by a skirt." This made him laugh out loud.

Further on, after he had zigzagged around another corner, a huge P.A. system had been blasting out U2's "Beautiful Day" at arena-like concert decibels. *I'm not sure what was more inspiring,* he said to himself. *The blasting speakers vibrating the city block, the music working the crowd's adrenaline, the runners feeding off the crowd's adrenaline or everything combined.* As he plodded on towards the mile sixteen marker, he couldn't help but wish that this was where the concert like experience had occurred.

He then thought back to a mile after passing what he called "U2's corner." A hip hop DJ had crafted his own visions of strength through speakers of similar power. *That bass beat was amazing… The thump and what it did for me. It was hard not to run at the tempo it was putting out,* Mitch said to himself. *I'm psyched that it was a fast tempo! But not so fast that I couldn't read the signs people around the DJ booth were holding.* He let the imagery of what he called "hip hop corner" play out in his mind as he crossed the sixteen mile mark. *"Run BITCH" was definitely my favorite sign,* he said to himself. *Nope… I definitely wouldn't see a sign like that during a race in Maine.*

As Mitch's body started to feel the miles he had already covered, he did his best to draw additional inspirations from earlier in the race… When he had felt invincible. He next recalled what happened about a mile after "hip hop corner." The course had taken the runners around a few tight turns and onto a narrow street where the crowds were stacked five people deep on both sides of the street. The skyscrapers were at least fifty stories tall and had created a huge reverberation tunnel from the thousands of cheering spectators. The cheers had been deafening. Each runner's laughter had been swallowed up by the frantic screams. *That's what a professional ballplayer must feel like when taking the field for the first time,* he thought to himself. *Only a big race does that to us amateur folks. What a rush!*

And to then see and hear Dylan amongst all those cheering people, he said to himself. *It was likely impossible, but I thought I heard her over the rest of the people when she had screamed "Go Mitch!"* The runner held the brief memory. *It was so great to see her there… To catch her eye and scream back at her "I love you!"… Even if it was just for a few seconds before I past her and raced on.*

As sixteen miles of racing fatigue began to invade his muscles, the runner looked at his watch. He quickly realized that it was only a few minutes after looking at it since the last time. *That didn't happen early in the race,* he said to himself. He remembered looking down at his watch for the first time in what seemed to be minutes after the start of the race and had almost toppled over when he saw that he had been running for over fifty five minutes.

Soon after adjusting to the time warp he had been in, he had passed the eight mile mark. *And that's when I gauged my pace against the pace guide Dyl wrote on my arm.* He remembered doing some math and noting to himself that he had been running way faster than he had planned. *That wasn't smart,* he said to himself. *But I was having way too much fun to be smart.*

So early in the race, Mitch's joy and elation of being around such positivity had won over all sense of reason and good judgment; he couldn't help but to push himself at an expedited pace. He had reminded himself that just a short hour before the start, he had been tired and questioning his motivation. How silly that all had been to him as the early part of the big-race experience had energized him, filled him to the rim with gratitude, and had him in full command of his task at hand. *Funny how mile eight felt. I can't remember ever feeling so good, so in control of myself, and so confident.*

He then reflected to when he had crossed the 20K marker. *It seemed like seconds later I rounded another turn and spotted the thirteen point one mile split sign... The halfway point!* The lighted clock letting the runners know how fast they were running had been glowing in the buildings' shadows on the side of the course. Just ahead of it had been the hydration aid station. About twenty feet beyond the water tables had been Matt, Pam, Ty, and Dylan. *1:37,* Mitch had told himself as he recalled running past the half marathon point. *Seven minutes faster than the pace written on my arm, yet I still felt fantastic.*

"Gatorade first, water second," the volunteers at the aid station had been chanting. Mitch had slowed, gulped down a chilled Gatorade, thanked the volunteers for being there, and raced down the street towards his friends and wife. He had first made a beeline towards Dylan as she snapped closer and closer photos of him, each image displaying a wider smile as he ran closer. After a huge kiss had been exchanged between them, he raised his hand over his head to deliver to Matt, in what Matt exclaimed to Mitch after the race, the hardest and most painful high five he had ever received. Leaving his wife and friends behind, he couldn't help but feel as if an incredible force of positive energy had taken over his soul. *And then I moved on to tackle the second half of the race. The hard part.*

He rolled his recent memories around in his head. He felt his body unintentionally slow down a little as he did this. *Everything was perfect. I ran a kick ass half and my confidence was greater than ever… But now… Shit. Stuff feels like it's starting to get out of my control.*

A little over three miles after causing Matt to ice the palm of his hand, the runner again looked at the warmer than usual sun which had crested over the three story apartment buildings. Moreover, humidity and its un-evaporative feel began to creep up along with the rising sun.

Mitch couldn't help but to then try and recall the moment in the race when he had noticed, in what seemed like a blink of an eye, there were no longer hordes of runners around him. *There used to be a lot of shadows on the ground in front of me, he told himself. Where are they?* He knew the question he asked himself was rhetorical, just as he knew why the pack was thinning out.

His mind inevitably replayed witnessing the quitting woman, her energy drain, and the ease in which she simply gave up. The only way he thought he could stop the sudden negative spiral he found himself in was to say aloud, "Not me… Not in this race!"

Beyond his control, however, an imaginary small, evil, floating being, the same one who had visited Mitch at last year's New York City Marathon, took up residence just off the runner's shoulder.

"How long can you keep this pace up?" the illusion whispered into Mitch's ear as it leaned in over the runner's shoulder. The entity spoke into his ear the same way a second grade boy tells a similarly aged girl that he holds a secret.

What the hell is he doing here so early in the race? The last time I saw him, it was after I passed the twenty three mile marker in NY. Panic raced down his spine. *I didn't think he'd appear for at least another seven or eight miles!*

The sinister floating demon continued, "Remember how tired your body felt when you woke this morning? Dude! You worked your ass off and recorded a full length CD this week. Now you expect to finish a marathon at a 7:40 pace while this heat and humidity are kicking in? C'mon, who are you kidding?"

The course took its next turn onto a main road and into the direct fullness of the hot sun. Fighting back his negativity with all the power he had, Mitch spoke through determined, squinted eyes. *I got this,* was his silent answer.

The widened course soon became an exposed four lane highway. The road headed out towards the huge expanse of the United Center and her open, treeless parking lots. As the growing intensity of the sun's brightness helped to kick up the temperature a few more notches, Mitch did his best to manifest the melting of the talkative, imaginary devil who had somehow taken a firm hold on his shoulder. For the moment, the hot sun liquefied the cunning imp, but only at the price of the day's first feelings of dehydration and tightness in his hard working hamstrings.

A mile later, the course took the athletes further south and brought them towards the south branch of the Chicago River. Protection from the sun was a limited commodity here as the runners ran past Industry's short and sprawling office buildings, vast warehouses, and empty truck parking lots. Much quieter than close to the downtown area, the sounds of dispersed cheering spectators continued to do their best to push the runners on. Above the softened volume of the thinned out cries of enthusiasm, Mitch began to notice the sounds of rubber grinding on the pavement; they were the same "screee… screee… screee…" sounds his shoes would make when, on a long run, he would bide his time by kicking an acorn down the road. This same sound, sadly to those who were experiencing it, was also the sound of tired legs not being able to pick up the feet they were connected to.

A quick glance by Mitch to his left displayed a man running with a tired and hunched over gate. A look right, he saw a few more tired runners. His next glance, this one ahead of him, filled him with envy as several friends he had been running with for the past two plus hours seemed to glide away from him. The sight left Mitch with the reality that he was no longer covering the same distance per stride as earlier in the race.

Oh man, c'mon body… We need to keep it up … Only seven or so miles left, he said to himself as the relentless struggle between his mind and body commenced. *Why is this happening? I've been running so great so far!*

There's a point in the marathon which every experienced endurance runner knows all too well. Each runner trains long, trains hard, and does everything in one's power to avoid this point, the instant where the body doesn't want to work the way the mind wants it to. During a marathoner's training, each runner continuously plays with training techniques, diet options, and whatever else might lie in one's bag of tricks in order to insure the body will hold up at mile twenty two, twenty four, twenty six point one.

Start fast? Start slow? Hold back in the beginning and give it your all at the end of the race? Or rip it hard in the beginning and hope the body holds up through twenty six point two miles? These questions are often repeated by athletes around the world. The beauty of the marathon, as well as its frustration, is that race day is the only time one knows how well their training approach works. For most endurance athletes, if a specific approach ends up not working, it's too late to change by the time they realize it. One can only hope, assume, or use an experienced educated guess that their race strategy will pay off to its fullest benefit on race day.

In an idealistic race, the starting horn blasts its long and loud tone; no countdown precedes the blast. The sound surprises each runner and supplies the morning's last nervous jitters in each runner's belly. Thousands of athletes take a deep breath together and tell themselves and each other "Here we go!" It's an amazing experience. The runners resonate from the power of the collective energy around them. As they move forward, they do their best to harness its power to feed their endurance through the distance. Each athlete is convinced that their body will rise to the occasion, their mind will provide the needed motivational stamina, and the heart will insure a speedy and pain free finish.

But the marathon is not one of these idealistic races. In short, it's difficult. Whether one is an elite athlete racing for a place on the podium or an amateur marathoner simply looking to finish better than the last time they ran, it's never easy. Again and again, the endurance runner tweaks their training approach to make the distance seem easier, and again and again, it's just plain hard.

Mitch thought about this for a few moments. Just a few hours ago, when he had looked into his eye's reflection, he had accepted that today's race might not be *his* race, yet he did his best to motivate past this fact. *I felt so good at the start,* he said to himself. *And I felt better at the half! Maybe I should have taken Dylan's advice and just had fun with this…"*

What seemed like days, but was only two and a half hours ago, when he had left Dylan in the athlete's village, she had said to him, "It's going to get hot. Start slow. Take in the experience. Conserve your energy. Adjust your pace for the heat. Finish strong. So what if you don't PR. Look what you're about to do. Have fun with this!" But, like all who are competitive, having fun wasn't an option. When the horn went off, Mitch went for it.

Mile twenty came and went. He looked at his watch. He wasn't happy. He tried his best to come to terms with his depleting energy level. *Damn heat! Damn studio time! I think I'm finally beginning to feel how much I actually put into the CD*, he admitted. *And the heat isn't helping...* His panic notched up one more level. *I had to go for it... I'm an athlete! I can't "just have fun." I* had *to push it!*

For twenty miles, pushing it had been the right choice. Unfortunately, for Mitch, this was a twenty six point two mile race. Prematurely depleted, it was too late for him to go back on his choice.

At first it was the little things which, after running for over two and a half hours, became incredible annoyances. *Why didn't I wear sunglasses?* the runner yelled at himself. *I know... I know. The prism effect of wet sunglasses*, he confessed as he recalled running through a spectator's improvised roadside sprinkler system during last summer's ninety degree 10K. *Water and sweat on the lenses hurt my eyes*, he continued. *Sunglasses during summer races don't work for me... So I went straight to Maine Running Company and bought my running hat.*

He moved on for a few moments at a slowing pace. *A lot of good my glasses are doing me sitting in my finisher bag... And this isn't supposed to be a summer race!* As he thought this last thought, he looked up at the eaves of the short buildings, squinted at the sun, and scorned it for being just two feet above what would be the safe protection of shadow.

The course made another left turn and again paralleled the river and the industrial train tracks it ran next to. Shade was difficult to come by. The athlete's legs desperately tried to keep up with his mind's motivation to keep on pace. Squinting through his pain, he made out at a distance the twenty-one mile marker. *Chinatown,* he said to himself. *I promised myself I wouldn't fall victim to the Great Wall of Chinatown... Damn!*

Mitch didn't hate many things. "Hate is such a strong word," he would often say. But when considering what's described when running marathons as The Wall, hate seemed to be an appropriate word. Ever since racing his first marathon, he would often hear more experienced runners, over and over, talk about the specific time in an endurance race when the body just doesn't have any more to give; primary muscles stop working and glycogen stores – the body's fuel – run out. *When the race becomes all mental because everything hurts. When the body needs the mind's help to climb over The Wall.*

One reason a marathoner trains so hard is to avoid even getting to the point when The Wall exists. A runner who approaches the marathon's distance to run a PR will run as many twenty-plus mile training runs their schedule can accommodate. The athlete will do their best to trick their body into feeling that twenty six point two miles is an achievable race distance. But running training runs and racing at one's best effort are two different things. If circumstance – rest during race week, injuries are kept in check, good running weather on race day – all work to a runner's favor, The Wall has a chance of being avoided. But when circumstances beyond control work against an athlete's goal, *That's when the wheels fall off the car,* Mitch said to himself.

As the runner turned down Wentworth Avenue and towards the twenty two mile marker, he began to feel small, random spasms of cramping in his legs. He knew that in a few minutes, he would be in pain, miserable, and might not be able to run. *I hate when the lactic acid bomb explodes in my legs. Shit!*

He winced and cursed his body. He knew his only tool to push him past his hurt and to a strong finish was positive thinking. But as the small spasms grew in number and began to turn his legs into lead bricks, positivity became the furthest thought from his consciousness.

"Really?" the deteriorating athlete asked himself out loud. *Please don't do this now. I'm four and a half miles away from finishing my fastest marathon. Please don't do this.* He continued to plead with his body. *I put in so much work to avoid this. Why is this happening?*

His appeal to his body went unanswered. The pain in his quads increased with the same vibrancy of a million dominos falling over. A quarter mile later, the discomfort plateaued for a brief moment and offered an ounce of hope that he might be able to push past the cramps. However, like fireworks going off a mile in the sky and the boom lagging behind the glowing stars of gunpowder, a delayed explosion of liquid fire surged through each muscle in his legs. The aftermath left a steaming, hardened trail of stone in its wake. As his legs stopped working, similar to the way a blown engine will clank, smoke, sputter, and die, the runner had no choice but to give in. *Fuck*, was all he could answer with.

Mitch stopped in the middle of the course. He took some labored breaths. He pushed himself to walk. *If I don't move forward, I have no chance of getting my legs back.*

He looked around. He noticed several other runners going through the same thing he was. A few were even talking to each other about their pain, the heat, their inability to go on, and their desire to quit. *Never surround yourself with negative people for they only bring you down. I gotta get away from these runners!*

Unfortunately for Mitch, there was a race-day glitch in his philosophy. Deep into the race, when the cancer of negativity began to resonate collectively from all the tiring athletes around him, it became very difficult for him to obey his own commands. Though he couldn't come up with the answer as to why, the more he tried to outrun the negativity around him, the more his legs resisted and decided they didn't want to work anymore.

Ever so slowly, he slogged past the twenty two mile marker. Next to the big square sign, which let him know that he had only four point two miles left to run, stood one of the official time clocks. He took note of the time, looked down at the pace schedule written on his arm, and did some did some impromptu math. What his calculations disclosed was that somehow, over the last two miles, he had gone from a projected PR pace to a no chance in hell you're gonna PR pace. *Like salt in the wound…* he said to himself. *The whole damn shaker.*

As the molten rock continued to harden in his quads, the shattered athlete couldn't come to terms with what was happening. *I told myself The Wall wasn't gonna stop me this time!* But no matter how hard or loud he reprimanded himself, the pain worked him down quicker and more efficiently than a gun at a sword fight.

Hydrate! I need to hydrate more. Electrolytes. That'll get me past this, he rationalized.

Beyond his control and expectedly unwelcome, the runner's evil counter ego reappeared. "Yeah right," said the uninvited hallucination. "You know it's past that point. Can't you feel the heat? You're already dehydrated and gone. Just stop and get a ride to the finish."

Mitch knew that he couldn't will the overly annoying imagination from his shoulder this time. He was too spent. But he also knew that listening to its negative banter was a choice. His choice. Decision made, he continued shuffling along at his slow, pained, and lethargic pace. *No way in hell I'm quitting*, he said to himself.

A half mile later, but what seemed like an eternity to Mitch's thirst-ridden and depleted body, he approached one of the late race hydration stations. He saw tables full of life-giving liquids in cups stacked four high with pieces of cardboard separating the rows. *That's one way to hydrate fifty thousand runners*, he said to himself. Slowing to a walk, he heard the familiar voices of the volunteers, "Gatorade first, water second…"

With tired hands, Mitch first reached for a Gatorade. He brought the cup to his lips and gulped. As it careened down his throat, he had to fight off the sudden urge to gag. *Warm… And they forgot to stir this batch… sun-baked, thick Gatorade paste. Nasty!* he thought while fighting back the urge to throw it all up.

He heard his little friend laugh in his ear. It was an evil giggle. "You should have been drinking the cold ones," said the hallucination. "I bet if you had stayed on pace, the sun wouldn't have had time to heat up these drinks. Serves you right! Just quit. It's much easier."

Mitch, again, through strength that he didn't know he had, chose to ignore what he was imagining. He walked past the Gatorade tables and to the water tables. *Even if the water isn't cold, there won't be any slurry at the bottom of the cup to deal with.*

Minutes later, after chasing down the thickness in his throat with multiple cups of warm water, his belly settled back to some semblance of normalcy. He thanked the volunteers at the table, took a long and deep breath, and on slow and heavy appendages that seemed to set a new universal record for their atomic weight, he moved on.

Mile twenty three seemed like an eternity to reach. *I feel like I should book a motel room in between the mile markers*, he joked with himself. *Maybe then I'll feel rested.* He was surprised his imaginary friend didn't jump on the opportunity to insist he do just that. *Is it because the water and Gatorade are starting to work their magic? Maybe?*

The runner felt a slight sense of hope. *Just keep it up until the next hydration station. Keep it up!* He told himself. He rounded the next corner onto Thirty Third Street. His hopefulness was short lived as the sun's full wrath hit him directly in his face. The quick blast of additional heat bore into his mind. With each step, he ripped further apart at his seams.

As his body broke down further, each article of clothing became an incredibly wet and sweaty annoyance. Every repeated arm and leg movement added to his suddenly painful chafes. His salty sweat intensified the pain in his well worn areas. His watch instantly became so irritating on his wrist that it felt as if he had spontaneously broken out from a sudden allergic reaction to poison ivy. His eyes continued to plead with his mind to stop and buy pair of sunglasses. His body petitioned the smiling folks in the crowd for a fresh set of legs.

It was obvious to Mitch now. The wheels had fallen off the car. *Run... Can't do this anymore! Walk... Count to twenty... Run at twenty... Go... Wait, just ten more seconds of walking... Go... Try to keep going... Don't quit. What mile is this? Can't do this anymore! Walk... Why? Why am I doing this? Hurts... Hurts... Just run... Where am I? Can't do this anymore! Walk...* The runner's overheated brain seemed to be stuck in an endless survival loop.

Mile twenty four soon caught his eyes. *Once I'm there, there's only two point two miles left,* he said to himself, followed by his best efforts to boost his confidence. *I've run twenty four miles. So close to finishing. Stay with it! Just don't look at the clock. Don't do it.*

But like a rubber-necker who can't resist looking at a bad car accident, he gave in. He looked up at the official display on the mile marker clock. His sight then focused down to the pace times on his arm. After doing the math, he was forced to come to grips with the truth and certainty of his race. *How can a race which I looked so forward to and trained so hard and tirelessly for end up being such a slow and painful experience? How?*

The realization seemed to finally get the better of him. Disheartened, the runner slowed, walked to the side of the course, and stopped. A few labored breaths later, he raised his head, squinted into the sun, and shed a tear. Not a tear of sadness, but pain, hurt, and ego. He had failed himself.

Mitch stood like this for what seemed an eternity. He watched hundreds of runners run, shuffle, or slog by him. He was beaten. Done.

His shouldered evil companion laughed at the ease in which the runner quit. "See how easy that was?" He asked through his gasps of laughter. Mitch did his best to suppress the mockery of it all. He understood that his attempt to hit his best marathon time was now a thing of the past. Frustrated and hurt by how the race had turned out, something deep inside him instructed him to take control over the things he could control; to make the rational choice to not quit, but to continue.

I'm a runner, he said to himself. *I'm slow, I'm hurting, but I'm an athlete. And I don't quit. I know this about myself. I've never quit anything before. I'm not gonna start now!*

The passing seconds ticked on to minutes. Mitch didn't care. Getting his body to move forward was his only care. *I'm a runner,* he again said to himself. *Run.*

Silence ensued in his mind as he gazed around at the cheering crowds. He made eye contact with spectators on the sides of the course. He could see their mouths scream "Go Mitch!" but it was as if someone had pressed the mute button on his internal remote.

He next reminded himself, *Dylan is at the finish. You can't leave her waiting for you. You know that she'll be worried sick if you don't show up.* He let this thought sink in.

The crowd's cheers began to break through the barrier his ego had erected. *So what… You're having one of those days,* he pleaded with himself. "Go Mitch" penetrated the silence. *Go Mitch,* he joined in with the crowd's cheers. *I'm so glad Dylan wrote my name on my shirt. She knew I'd need the help. I need to finish. For Dylan.*

He took a step forward, caught himself from stumbling, stopped, and then took another step. The 3:30 pace group zoomed by him. *Ha! I was supposed to beat them*, Mitch sarcastically said to himself and laughed. He then found himself surprised that he had the energy to even laugh at all.

"Every strong runner has fallen apart during a marathon at one point in their running lives. Stop the fucking drama, Mitch! Finish!" he said out loud.

"Go Mitch" was now resonating in his skull. The runner looked up. Random strangers were doing their best to push him on. He nodded to each one he saw yelling his name. *All right... I'm in!* he telepathically said to them, and moved forward with a renewed goal to simply complete the distance.

He walked. His walk then progressed to a slow shuffle. He did his best to utilize his arms in order to create some forward momentum. *One step at a time,* was his next thought as he took inventory of his cramped and weakened body. "Take your time, Mitch," he continued in a whisper. "Make it to Dylan. It's just a race. There will be others. Just get to her."

He imagined finally kissing his wife. With his ego free from the confines of hitting a goal time coupled with how great it was going to feel when he finally made it to Dylan, his body relaxed. Cramps began to dissipate. His shuffle became more of a jog. He made his arms act like pistons in his best hopes to relieve some of the burden from his weary legs. His legs finally did what he had begged them to do earlier. Albeit slowly, he was running.

And I'm gonna finish this damn thing running. The goal to be with Dylan at the finisher party became his mind's primary focus. *I'm not failing*, Mitch continued. *I'm running. I will always run,* the athlete said to himself through tears of exhaustion. *I'm a runner... And I'm gonna finish like one.* After all he had put his mind and body through, finishing as a runner was just fine with him.

As the course further took the athletes up Michigan Avenue and towards the finish, the hot sun permeated the sky directly down onto the exposed four lane city highway. The runners passed a shadowed electric time and temperature sign mounted on the side of a brick building. Mitch took notice and watched the sign blink from 10/10/10 to 10:36AM to 88 degrees. *What did that say?* He asked himself. He was already comfortable with running slow and decided to slow his jog a little more so he could be sure that what he saw wasn't a trick of the light. Sure enough, when the temperature reading came back around, it was pegged at 88 degrees. *So that's why I'm feeling the way I do*, he rationalized. *Well, one of the reasons I feel the way I do… Whatever. I don't care.*

He ran with his new, simple goal helping him to escape from his mind. He floated above himself, finally finding The Zone. He let his body work. He let his body run for the sake of running.

He soon fell in stride with and even passed a few other runners. Less than an hour ago, Mitch would have been psyched about propelling past other marathoners at the end of a long race. At this point, in this race, it didn't matter.

"Good job," was muttered in a slurring voice from his tired lips as he passed other runners. He became confused that he had just past runners while jogging at a pace that he compared to the speed of magma flowing uphill. *Just keep running… Finish… Make it to Dylan.*

He came upon the race's final hydration station at mile twenty five point two. Mitch opted for water, thanked the volunteers, made some more eye contact with his fellow running friends taking a drink, and continued to push his slow pace towards the finish. *One mile left… Just twice around the horse track. Easy!*

He made the right turn onto Roosevelt Road. Mile marker twenty six was soon upon him. *A thousand feet left…* he yelled to himself. He made the quick hard left turn onto Columbus

Drive. The finisher's area was right in front of him. He kept his pace slow and cool. He noticed the spectator bleachers filled with roaring fans and families of runners. Time seemed to slow down. Life seemed like an illusion to him.

Mile twenty six point one came and went. *500 feet!* He yelled to himself. In the near distance, finally, he made out the finish line. To Mitch, this last one tenth of a mile was a relaxed dream. He effortlessly passed a few more runners and let himself be passed by others. He took notice of the fans in the bleachers cheering, shaking their cowbells, and banging their thunder sticks together. In his dreamlike state, each spectator seemed to take on the persona of a cartoonist's washed out rendition of a sports fan. *Like characters in a Picasso painting.*

Two hundred fifty feet left. He looked up at the huge clock over the finish line, innocently revealing to him that he had been on this journey for three hours and forty eight minutes. *It's all good,* he rationalized. *I'm here. I beat the negative. I made a choice not to give in… And I didn't. I'm going to finish this thing running.*

Mitch slowly continued forward. *Fifty feet left…* he said to himself. He held his head high. He accepted his finish time with the same honest persistence which had gotten him here. He acknowledged that he had pushed his muscles way beyond his known ability to push them, and they didn't fail him. He took pride in his beaten mind which had bounced back from the depths of quitting again and again. With a heart invigorated by his love for life, Dylan, and running, he crossed the finish line.

Once across, he didn't raise his arms in the air with a sense of accomplishment, nor did he shout out about the glory in his achievement the way some of his fellow runners celebrated. Quietly, without fanfare, he just stopped running.

He stopped running.

A few steps later, he lowered and then raised his head. He inhaled some warm, fresh air and gave himself a small pat on his left shoulder with his right hand. As he did so, he told himself *Great job. I'm a runner. I finished running. I rock.*

Once inside the finisher chute, he lined up behind runners who had finished before him in order to receive his finisher's medal from one of the volunteers. He thanked the volunteer who placed a medal around his neck and proceeded to give her a hug.

A few steps later, he was offered an emergency blanket from another volunteer; the kind of blanket one puts around them to prevent hyperthermia from kicking in. "Really?" he said to the man holding the shiny metallic disposable blanket up for him. "Well, it is October in Chicago," he sarcastically answered, followed by the truthful statement, "It was fifty degrees at this time last year!"

Mitch let the volunteer hold onto his allotted blanket and moved past him. He had one more thing left to do and one more mile to go in order to accomplish it. This last mile, likely one of the longest miles he would ever travel in his life, opened itself up to him with wide arms. The athlete let himself become embraced by it.

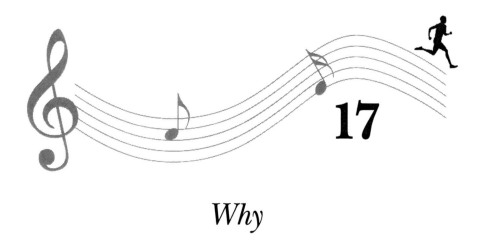

Why

"Cold beer?" The voice shook Mitch from his walking trance. The word cold brought amazing tingles to his dry and cotton-mouthed pallet. *And did he say beer?* he asked himself. Though the runner loved beer, he couldn't quite grasp that this would be his first post-race beverage.

Mitch looked up and saw a "Goose Island Brewery" cart manned by a smiling volunteer. He was handing out glistening frosty cups to passing finishers. Each runner who passed the cart smiled, took a beverage – because it was cold, first and foremost – and slowly moved on. Mitch did the same.

The delightful feeling from the chilled cup on the palm of his hand seemed to take his breath away. The runner wanted to hug this man so badly. Fortunately for the vendor, he was able to escape Mitch's sweaty embrace by helping out other exhausted runners.

After a small sip teased his cotton-mouth for the moment, Mitch rested the side of the cup on the back of his neck with the hopes of cooling all the blood flowing to and from his hazy brain. *So good. Thank you Universe for cold things on hot days.*

After a few dreamy moments of embracing the cup of beer in ways it was never intended to be embraced, the runner ran the cup across his face for comfort before bringing the beverage to his lips and letting a small amount of the cooling magic flow down his throat and into his belly. As he sipped, he couldn't help but imagine a Rocky Mountain waterfall during springtime runoff.

He drank a quarter of the beer in small sips. Since alcohol wasn't a very good idea for a dehydrated and beaten athlete, he decided to pour the rest of the cup out. *There will be time for this later.* After a burp and a smile, he continued to walk with his fellow finishers towards the Twenty Seventh Mile Post-Race Party, where he'd finally see Dylan.

Though some complained about having to walk almost another mile to get to their friends and family, most of the runners knew why the Race Directors made everyone do such a long post-race walk. Aside from preventing the cramping of now under-utilized muscles, it was also a way to ensure there would be no bottleneck at the finish line. In order to spread tens of thousands of runners out, the only logical thing to do with them was to keep them moving forward. Even though it made sense, each runner's feet hurt so badly. When coupled with the collective desire to just sit down and rest, it became amazingly difficult for everyone to push on. But each runner did.

A quarter of a mile later, on the other side of the fence Mitch was walking next to, he noticed a small crowd surrounding multiple canvas booths. Each tent had a label on the front corresponding to the bib numbers the runners wore. An explosion of happiness hit Mitch as he realized that, in just a few minutes, he'd be on the other side of this fence picking up his finisher bag… The bag that held his sunglasses. *I'm finally going to be able to stop squinting*!

The herd of athletes approached the barrier gate at the end of the long finisher chute. One by one, they slowly went through the five foot opening and towards their respective finisher bag pickups. With such a slow exit, runner traffic started to back up at the gate. A little closer to the chute's exit, Mitch noticed the cause of the traffic: A few hundred overly enthusiastic spectators who wouldn't wait for the twenty seventh mile to reconnect with their loved ones were blocking the exit.

"We know you want to see your friends and family and congratulate them, but please stand aside and let the runners through the gate," said an officer into a megaphone. "They've been on their feet long enough. They don't need to be stuck in a traffic jam."

"Thank you," Mitch said to the directing officer as he walked past him.

"My pleasure," said the officer. "Congratulations on breaking four hours!"

Mitch smiled back. *All things considered, I did do well.*

As fantastic as it would have been to see Dylan here, he knew that she and their friends would be in Grant Park, now only a half mile away. Knowing they'd be waiting patiently at the light pole which bore the letter "A," corresponding to his last name, helped him to stay focused and positive about his still unfinished goal.

He rounded the gate, made his way into the tent city, and found his respective group of numbers hanging on the front of a canvas tent. He got in line behind a few runners and waited for thirty seconds. Once it was his turn, a volunteer noted the bib number still pinned to the front of his shirt, turned, grabbed his bag, and handed it to him.

"Congratulations!"

"Thank you," Mitch replied through his smile. "In this bag is one of the best rewards possible!"

As he spoke, he reached into his bag, pulled out his sunglasses, and put them on. "Ohhhh, bliss," involuntarily rolled off his lips.

The volunteer smiled and said, "Bet those were needed about two hours ago!"

Mitch nodded. "Man, was I dumb for keeping them here," he said. "But it's all good now."

Noting other runners behind him, Mitch stepped aside and out of the way of the tent booth. He took a look into his bag and saw the amazing, dry-cotton extravaganza of clothes he had packed for himself to change into. *And I packed my flip flops, too! Those are gonna feel* so *good on my beat feet.*

Efforts to fight off the urge to change into his dry clothes and flip flops seemed equal to keeping a hungry dog from devouring a cooked prime rib sitting in his bowl. But he held back. *I gotta get to Dylan first. Once I sit down, I don't think I'll be able to get up!* Finisher bag in hand, sunglasses over his eyes, and walking on the now wider road towards the celebration in the park, he moved on with slow and deliberate speed.

As Mitch walked on, he noticed the abundant number of finishers had thinned out. Now out of the barrier area and free to do what they wanted, some eagerly sat down amongst the shady trees which lined the road. Others, who were already reunited with their friends and loved ones, also sat down and finally relaxed.

With fewer people walking on the road, it was easy for Mitch to take notice of a homemade oak tag banner stapled to a four foot garden stick. It was leaning against one of the roadside trash cans in a way that seemed to know Mitch would be there to walk by it.

"Pain is temporary. Pride is forever," was the banner's message. These six words eloquently described the grueling endeavor which he had just put himself through. *Pain is temporary. Pride is forever,* he repeated. *I've seen that banner a hundred times… But it was never as true as it is today.*

Involuntarily, tears began to fall from behind his sunglasses. The runner felt chills run up his spine and out to his extremities as he did his best to pull himself together, but the mantra had hit him hard. It made him painfully aware of just how fragile he was, no matter how strong he considered himself to be.

He again re-read it. The emotion flowed from his eyes while seeming to simultaneously explode from his entire body.

I finished. I finished still able to run. I didn't succeed in my original goal, but I've embraced what became a new goal, and now I'm just minutes away from fulfilling it. He paused and countered... *But am I giving myself an easy out instead of admitting that I failed myself?* He pondered this, and continued.

Rationalizing won't make me stronger, but learning from my mistakes will. I think I just need to give it some time before I really understand what I've learned. He thought about this for a bit and then admitted to himself, *I'm not rationalizing... I'm growing... And accepting the process. That's something I can be proud of.* More tears fell from his eyes. *Pride is forever. It's time to find Dylan!*

He took one huge long breath and then another. He turned and walked further down the road towards the post-race music. A few steps further, he again said to himself, *Time to find Dylan.*

Though he had already made the conscious decision not to pick apart his race, walking seemed to activate the cogs in his brain. Reflections bloomed over the next half mile, regardless of how much he tried not to think about what he had just been through. He utilized his alone time to compare how his approach to the race was similar to the way he looked at life. He listed each lesson as matter of fact, without melody, without force, spoken instead with a competitor's conviction.

I got my ass kicked today and then I kicked ass, was the first thought to surface.

I'm blessed with loving a woman who loves me to the deepest realm of my core. And I love her that much more. A few more tears began to run down his already salty cheeks.

His thinking and walking moved forward simultaneously. "I've learned that I can enjoy the fitness my training brings me. It helps me sing. And singing helps my running," he said out loud before going silent for a few moments.

He inhaled a few more relaxing breaths. "And I'm definitely going to race another marathon. That goes without saying," nodding as he whispered this statement. "From the first day of training to the moment I cross the finish line, there's so much I learn about myself." With these thoughts leaving his lips, he felt as if he were running again.

Amongst the thin parade of chatting finishers, he continued to walk towards the park in reflective silence. *Those things are all great, but how do I tie it all together?* he thought to himself. *My training, the CD, the race, everything I've learned over the last four months and especially from this past week...*

Memories of the ups and downs of his training journey, balancing tireless days of running and music, singing endless vocal takes over the past week, his race meltdown, and how he chose to react to both the good and bad experiences of the past four months bombarded his mind. With each additional step, his forward momentum seemed to assist with bringing the pieces of this puzzle closer together... And then it hit him.

"Choice..." he whispered. "Happiness is all about choice."

Mitch felt his shoulders drop. He involuntarily arched his back and held his head high. He laughed to himself as he thought about the choices he'd made and the pride he finally accepted.

This whole week has been the greatest experience of my life. I've combined my love of music, my love of fitness, my love of competition, and my love of life. And now I get to go see Dylan.

"I'm so damned fortunate!" That, he couldn't help but say out loud. He smiled big enough to feel the sunshine reflect off his teeth and melt some of the steel that had hardened his face throughout the day.

The music from the park began to get louder and clearer as he approached. *Not much further now.* He made out the road's end and the concrete pillars that welcomed people into the park. A little bit closer, and he was able to make out the post-race party's size... The hugeness of it all.

Approaching the opening to the field from the access road, he spotted the first light pole. About thirty feet off the ground, a huge rectangular sign saying "A," was mounted to it. *Having a last name that starts with "A" does have its perks.*

He moved towards the pole. He scanned left, right, and center as he walked. He did it again. And there she was. Though she was over a hundred feet away and the DJ's music was blaring over the acreage, when she locked her eyes on his, her "Oh, Mitch!" was heard delightfully clear by the runner. He was so blown away that he had to stop and convince himself that she was real.

Tears poured from his eyes. She jumped forward and ran towards him. He still couldn't move. He just stared. And cried.

And then she was in front of him, staring. Seconds later she was holding him. She cradled his beat up body. With her touch so real and his goal now complete, the runner finally let himself fall to the ground. And she fell with him. And she cried with him. Beyond any doubt, his race was now over. He felt so accomplished. And it was so sweet!

"Runner down! Runner down!" cried a voice from above them, too far away to be a person standing near them, but yet right there. When Dylan and Mitch looked up, they noticed the multitude of beach lifeguard stands scattered throughout the park. One was right next to them. Each stand was manned with a sharp-eyed EMT whose job was to let the medics on the ground know that an overheated and collapsed runner needed their assistance. Within seconds, four EMTs were surrounding them. Each medic was locked and loaded with a one gallon bag of ice ready to empty on the overheated runner's head.

Over the loud music, Mitch shouted in the most polite way he could, "I'm OK! Really. I'm OK. This is just an emotional breakdown. We're all good... Great, actually!" And then requested through tears and a smile, "But I'll gladly take a bag of ice, if that's OK with you guys." Each EMT couldn't resist smiling back. One at a time, they congratulated the runner and handed him an ice pack for each appendage.

With the medics gone and Mitch and Dylan alone in their own bubble with the magic of ice to comfort them on this amazingly hot day, they once again held each other's eyes.

"I think I would have run a little better if I was chewing on ice cubes the whole race," Mitch said sarcastically.

Dylan, with her knowledge of Mitch's finish time through the Athlete Alert app programmed into her cell phone, once again took his face into her hands and said, "You did amazing. It might not have been your fastest race, but it was definitely your strongest." She let the statement sit for a few seconds and then said, "I'm so proud of you."

Mitch felt his belly flutter with a high school sweetheart type of crush. "I'm so in love with you it's silly," he said. "Thank you."

And then they kissed. The two stopped for a quick moment, looked deep into each other's eyes, and kissed again.

Lips separated and deep breaths taken, Dylan looked down at how her husband was dressed and said, "Now let's get these running shoes off and get you out of these wet clothes!"

Mitch felt as happy as a two year old diving into a bowl of whipped cream. He crunched down ice cubes while Dylan unlaced his shoes and swapped them out with his comfy flip flops. "OK, up you go! Roll yourself up in your towel, strip, and we'll get some dry clothes on!"

Dylan rose, extended her hand, and helped Mitch get to his feet. Wrapped in his towel and displaying the grace of a ballerina with a broken leg, Mitch swapped out his running shorts for his soft cotton underwear and his favorite lazy shorts. After the change of his clothes was completed and the two were again seated, they heard, "Mitch! Dylan!" from a short distance away.

Matt was walking towards them with three beers clasped in hand. Tucked under one of his arms was a pair of inflatable thunder sticks. "Man, how the hell did you run in this heat?" Matt said as he approached them. "I'm dying just walking across the park!"

"I've got good grapple," the runner replied. This got Matt laughing.

Matt handed Mitch and Dylan a beer and let the thunder sticks fall to the ground.

"What are those?" Mitch asked as he pointed to the long inflated sticks on the grass.

"Oh, these?" replied Matt. "I've been annoying the hell out of everyone for the past four hours. Matt put his beer down. He picked up the thunder sticks, put one in each hand and looked at Mitch. Dylan rolled her eyes, knowing what was coming next.

"Check it out," said Matt as he raised the sticks over his head and started chanting "Runners! Runners!" and then clapped the two sticks together loudly with a rhythm similar to a home team drum beat clapped at baseball games, "Doom, doom, doom-doom-doom."

"They sound like a bad floor tom, but making noise with them is still fun," the engineer added as he chanted and banged the sticks together a few more times.

His display of enthusiasm over, Matt dropped the sticks to the ground and sat down next to his friends. He picked his beer off the ground, held it up to Mitch and Dylan's and said, "Congrats, Mitch! Congrats on the run and congrats on the CD. You did it!"

Plastic cups were clinked. Good beer slid down their throats. Mitch couldn't help but to smile. In his mind and by his own choice, he had accomplished a whole lot more than making a CD and completing a marathon. He grew.

"Where's Pam and Ty?" Mitch asked after swilling down more cold goodness.

"Oh," said Matt. "Pam stayed behind to nap Carter. Ty got called in to sub for a doubles tennis tournament. After watching the marathon, he was really psyched to play," he added as he sipped his beer. "It's just the three of us."

"Tis a beautiful thing!" Mitch said. "But the three of us around a restaurant table with burgers and Bloody Marys would be even more beautiful."

Dylan quickly answered the call by saying, "Then let's go!"

The three finished their beers. Dylan and Matt stood first and helped Mitch to his feet. After a few slow steps towards the park's exit, Mitch said, "I guess it's gonna be a long march to the restaurant, but I'll get there!"

"I don't doubt that," said Matt and then looked at Dylan. "Do you mind being Mitch's caretaker and helping him walk out of the park? I've got some more noise to make!"

"Not a problem," replied Dylan. She laughed at Matt's continued need to make noise, even though the runners he was cheering for had been done running for almost an hour. She looked at Mitch and saw that he was also laughing.

"Awesome!" exclaimed Matt as he took his thunder sticks from beneath his arm and began to cheer every finisher he saw… And there were thousands of them, each smiling and each a champion.

Mitch leaned on his wife's shoulder. He hobbled slowly towards the park's exit and the restaurant's gluttony. He relished in how good he felt, how empowered he was, and how much, at this very moment, he appreciated his life. He couldn't help but to pull Dylan closer as he thought to himself, *This is why I run*.

~coda~

March, 2012

My skis are perpendicular to the incredibly steep fall line, the steepest I've ever been on. From high up, just below Dodge's Drop, I'm looking across the vast bowl and huge headwall of Tuckerman Ravine, New Hampshire. Dangerous overhanging cornices cling to the headwall's lip. The smallest vibration would cause them to let go. On the left side of the headwall is an avalanche chute which let go... A few days ago? Last week? At the base of the chute is the debris field I'm really hoping no one had to dig themselves out of. No one could. My eyes adjust to the elevation difference between the base of the bowl and the summit of Mount Washington beyond. I'm suddenly experiencing instant vertigo. I quickly take care of the dizziness by bringing my vision back to what's directly in front of me: The craziest shit I'm ever going to attempt to ski!

"How you doing, Mitch?" Jeff asks me while he's using his avalanche shovel to dig a bench in the forty five degree slope so he can sit and attach his snowboard to his boots. He moves with the grace of a monkey swinging in a tropical forest's canopy.

"Wishing that I had as much experience in this terrain as you," I answer. "Those mountaineering boots are really that secure on this surface?"

"I gotta kick in pretty hard on an incline like this one. But once the boot's toe is in the top layer of the snowpack, these things are beasts!" Jeff answers. "And they turn out to be some pretty good snowboard boots, too."

I observe Jeff with envy. Compared to Jeff's rugged and stiff ice climbing/mountaineering boots, my telemark boots and their huge plastic duck billed toes – the part that clips me into my skis' bindings – are not the ideal climbing tools for such a steep incline.

During the climb, to kick my boots in, I seemed to have had to work two to three times as hard as Jeff. My plastic toes were no match for the hard pack compared to the way Jeff's heavy duty boots broke into the same crusty wall of snow.

And when the terrain got steeper than I had ever expected, kicking in no longer became an option for me. Each time I tried to get some purchase, the leg that was supporting me felt like it was going to slip and I'd be propelled down the fifteen hundred foot bowl and into its basin. I had to work it that much harder just to stop the sewing machine needle like spasms from happening in the leg which was tasked with keeping me from falling.

After a few very sketchy moments, I thought following in Jeff's tracks would be safer. But when I got into his tracks, the stride of his tall legs didn't match mine and made for an even more precarious climb. Moreover, after first ski-skinning up the three miles to the Hermit Lake cabin, my legs are pretty tired from then having to lash my skis onto my daypack and kick up the fifteen hundred vertical feet to where we are right now.

"You sure it's OK we didn't make it to the top of the bowl?" Jeff asks me. "I know I told you we'd get there, but now that you've told me how hard you had to work to climb this high, I'm not sure how safe it would be to try the icy conditions above us." He pauses, turns around, sits on his newly made snow bench, and begins to work at getting his snowboard off his daypack. "I feel bad we didn't make the summit after I promised you we would... When we started to climb, you were so psyched to make it to the ridge!"

"It's all good," I answer immediately. "Look at where we are! This is amazing! So what if there are a few hundred vertical feet above us that we can't ski." We both look above towards the fingers of rocky crags and the chutes of skiable snow which separate them.

I continue, "About a year and a half ago, I learned a trick to adjust my goals when fatigue kicks in or if conditions don't permit them to be attained." I pause for a few seconds to let the statement sink in. "When I omit failure, my only choice is happiness."

"Aren't you the philosophical skier," Jeff answers with a smile.

"Always," I reply through a smile of my own. "Besides, I'm about to take the craziest ski run of my life! No way I can be upset we didn't finish what we initially set out to do!"

"Well... Ski!" Jeff enthusiastically commands.

The first turn on a super steep slope is always the hardest.... But is also the sweetest.